# Woman
## with a
# Word

*Silence is not Golden*

## Sarah Speaks

Published by:

ISBN: - (paperback)

# Dedication

I dedicate this book to anyone who has been silenced by any means. It is time to break the silence. Silence is not golden.

YOU ARE NOT ALONE.

# Contents

# Little Penny

*Valuable little penny*
*Her share of despair is plenty.*
*Worthy yet deemed not,*
*A necessity yet forgot.*
*Overlooked and cast down*
*Used without consideration always passed around.*

*Stepped on, scooted out of the way*
*Many have dropped her with dismay.*
*They tried to steal her luster and shine*
*Though she has always been mine.*
*Covered in scratches she appears dull and dark*
*No dazzle left, not even a hint of her spark.*

*She looks as worn as she must feel*
*After all she has treaded places less than ideal.*
*Covered in filth the color is that of ash*
*My special treasure treated as trash.*

1

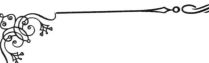

*Oh, valuable little penny.*
*Her share of despair is plenty.*
*Nothing can take her worth.*
*It is time for a re-birth.*

*Only He can remove her darkness.*
*"Come in, enter into His rest."*
*I am jealous for her.*
*I will cover her in hyssop and oils of myrrh.*
*Reminisce of yesterday no longer.*
*She is my warrior, more than a conqueror.*
*She belongs to me, my possession.*
*Everything I have done is for her*
*she is my obsession.*
*Persuasion tried swaying you towards not being valuable.*
*You are valuable beyond estimation, thoroughly invaluable.*

*My valuable little penny.*
*Her reward now is plenty.*

# Acknowledgments

First, I want to thank God for His amazing grace and for giving me the opportunity to share this portion of my story for His glory. He alone deserves the glory and the honor. He alone has kept me.

Secondly, I want to pay homage to my precious grandmother Bernice Mills. She transitioned during the perilous onslaught of the COVID- 19 global pandemic, but right before she did, we had a conversation that left an indelible mark on me. At one point in my life, she was a critic of my ministry, but she transformed into a commentator of my destiny. Her death birthed life into my first book.

I want to thank all my friends and family who have supported me on this journey; too many to name. You know who you are!

I must mention by name my supportive uncle Jeff Mills who contributed meaningfully to bringing this book to fruition and my dearest and most constant friend Michele Osborne. Michele and her family have loved me as their very own.

I recognize and highly honor the true men and women of God who have led me in the right direction— 'lighthouses' as I call them. A special thanks to Apostle Jefferson Stephen Okello. No matter the distance, he has been an example and a guide. I will forever be thankful.

To all my intercessors who have prayed me through some of the most difficult times of my life, I acknowledge you (some known I'm sure many unknown). I thank you. I honor you.

I acknowledge Hilette Virgo and Great Nest Publications for seeing the value in my story and helping me in the final moments of furnishing this book and bringing it to completion!

# Introduction

I was sweeping in a hurry one day when I briefly glanced and saw some type of coins mixed with the dust. Nonchalantly, I went to dump the dustpan when I heard the Holy Spirit say to me, "Don't throw that money away. It is still valuable."

I focused my gaze with intent to discover what money was in this pile of dust. Intermingled with the dirt and disposable things, I saw a few pennies. As I stared intently upon these beautiful yet dingy looking pennies, tears began to flow from my eyes as He began to speak again. He said, "Sarah you were that penny".

A strong conviction came into my heart as I pulled them out one by one and dusted them off. I placed them in my pocket, and from that day, He began giving me the message of 'VALUE being in the eyes of the beholder'.

Our viewpoints are meaningless without the insight of God's precious Holy Spirit. What we deem not valuable through the lens of natural sight—cluttered with judgment and opinions— are demolished when we are filled with His love, His Spirit and His Word.

I am reminded every time that I see pennies to find the value inside myself and others. I consider myself today to be a "Spiritual Numismatist". A numismatist is someone who studies and collects coins and other currency units. I can now see the value inside of His people no matter what the outside package looks like. I see much deeper within.

## My testimony

The payback is worth it. Until I had the ability of unobstructed vision with light as a guiding force leading the way, I stumbled blindly through wrong doors that darkness had to offer. Hopelessness was my deficiency. Faithlessness was my disease. Lovelessness was my dungeon.

Many weapons in the form of theft and death came in attempts to steal the very essence of my being. Torment and anguish took its toll on this tortured soul and battered body. Only upon confession and complete surrender to the light before me could I behold the very first and brightest glimpse of a shimmer of hope, faith, and love.

There was an unseen war raging and I was born right in the middle of it. I was a captive, a prisoner of war; unable to choose my own will. I needed a Savior.

Without enlightenment of my identity, I was easily enticed towards false narratives of acceptance and love. I was an abused, attention starved, love seeking addict. Marred by the wounds that the past had inflicted, my only motive in life was to try and stay hidden; exempting myself from the moment called the present.

Suppression was my defense and my weapon. I was kept hostage by the ideologies of other's perception of me—lies all lies. Misery consumed my soul. Endless repetitive cycles of insanity. Same results. Destruction met me at every dead end of these devilish paths I wandered down. Suicide always spoke to me, asserting itself to be the cure. Choices, so many choices; the voices of shame and regret followed the ones that I chose.

There is an unseen enemy of our lives. He has one purpose—armed with many tactics and devices. An ancient enemy with a clever skill set—cunning and baffling. The accuser. Adversary. Deceiver. Evil one. Thief. Tempter. Wicked one. Serpent of old. Fallen star. Murderer. Lawless one. Beast. Dragon. Father of lies. Prince of darkness. Devil. Satan. Lucifer. So many names but one plan—to steal, kill and destroy. Operating in so many lives; undetected, masked and cloaked in disguise. Wreaking havoc in attempts to deter us from the pursuit of the true and perfect plan.

Bound in shackles as a prisoner of this unseen war, I yielded and surrendered to the only One who could save me—my Jesus. The One who I had heard about in passing. The One who has always known me, but I never had the revelation of truly knowing Him. Salvation was my free pardon and release from the shackles I inherited from the first Adam.

This mystery of being created in Christ became my identity through the last Adam— my Savior. Redeemer. Rescuer. The Christ. Immanuel. Lord of lords. King of kings. Advocate. Bridegroom. Messiah. Mighty One. Wonderful Counselor. Mighty God. Everlasting Father. Prince of Peace. The way, the Truth and the Life. The One whom I sought after all my life and could not find in the world.

The world had tried to offer me imitations that I discovered to be counterfeit. Jesus, the fulfillment of all things not only within myself but the message to carry; the answer that everyone is seeking. The solution to every problem. The One they are running from.

I had tasted what the world had to offer. Bitterness and hatred were just a few of its flavors. I was empty and desolate always left longing for something else. Feeling impure, defiled, and damaged by the world. Disgusted with myself and the experiences I had encountered.

I wore shame like a coat. Intimidated and afraid of others. I was lashed by their words, beaten by their hands. Rejected and overlooked by so many; used and abused for momentary pleasure. After so much was taken, I did anything I could to become hidden—numb. I was taught to never speak for myself. Without a voice to cry out, I welcomed death. I was convinced that I was ruined, not broken. Something that is broken can be fixed. Something that is ruined cannot be repaired.

Even before the truth set me free, I was still His beloved and part of something far greater than my mind could conceive. Created on purpose. Chosen with a calling. Designed for pivotal destiny.

Royalty! I was a queen and did not even know it. I walked for far too long as a peasant. I did not possess truth. I walked down the treacherous paths but now I can share the power of redeeming love. A passionate desire that the Savior has for me and for you—His beloved. He is persistent, unchanging and yearns for you. You are the apple of His eye. He endured the shame of the cross for the joy that was set before Him. We are that joy, precious one, you and me.

I do not believe you are reading this by chance. I have prayed for you. I have petitioned the courts of heaven for you. I am touching and believing that you will glean something from what I have been commissioned to write. With all my love and sincere greetings, welcome!

# Chapter 1
# Womb to the world

*You formed my innermost being, shaping my delicate inside and my intricate outside, and wove them all together in my mother's womb.*

***Psalms 139:13 TPT***

I was born in the beautiful 'Mountain Momma' state also known as the wild and wonderful West Virginia. On May 26, 1986, my fight to live began. I was in the balance of teetering between life and death. This is my side of my life's story.

My grandmother was the one who noticed I was not breathing. At first, no one paid her a bit of mind. However, one thing about my 'mamaw' was this, you listened to what she had to say, one way or another. She saved my life. Her stern, strong and protective nature intervened that day preserved my life.

Soon after I was born, a snapshot was given to my mother in case she never saw me again. My lungs collapsed and were filled with fluid. To top it off, I was premature. The reports of the doctors were not good. I was life-flighted from Logan

Regional Hospital to Cabell Huntington Hospital Neonatal Unit where I was placed in an incubator for weeks monitored daily with I.V.'s and tubes sustaining my life.

My father was in high hopes of having a son that day. I was to be named Alexander. Deciding that my name was then the next obstacle to overcome—since Alexander was not very fitting—the next name in line was Alexandria. Still not settled with the name choice, my parents went on a quest to find me a fitting name.

There was a popular song entitled 'Sara Smile', sung by Daryl Hall & John Oates (my sister sang it all the time). That was the inspiration of how I was given my name. Sara with an 'h' at the end. A name that holds royal meaning; 'princess' in Hebrew.

I ended up being the healthiest baby in the NIC unit. I was born with thick black hair everywhere. For goodness sakes, I was told they had to shave me for all the lines and tubes to be placed in me. I earned a string of nicknames to include: daddy's little "sumo wrestler" (because I wound up growing to be chunky yet muscular at the same time), "Whitney Pooh" and my least favorite, "Monkey". Monkey is not one I wanted to share but for history's sake (and my sister's enjoyment) I am revealing.

# Chapter 2
## Kidnapped

*When you go through deep waters, I will be with you. When you go through rivers of difficulty, you will not drown. When you walk through the fire of oppression, you will not be burned up; the flames will not consume you.*

*Isaiah 43:2 NLT*

My father was an abusive, drug dealer and addict. What his life was like I do not know. I have lived off other people's memories of him coupled with glimpses of our times together—my first years on this earth and the two weeks before he died. There was a huge time gap in between which I will fill you in as you continue this journey with me.

When I consider my father's addiction, an example that comes to mind are the Dr. Jekyll and Mr. Hyde personalities. He was a dealer and user of drugs and alcohol, as well as a business owner.

I was two when it happened. Kidnapped—taken out of the country to be raised in a different culture and fed despairing lies. The reason behind it? Like I said, I lived off the reportage of others. I was told that, one, he did it to hurt my mother and two, he did it to protect me from my mother.

I strongly believe it was a mixture of both. Either way, the facts remain that I was taken to the country of Mexico where I spent my formative years. The cries and the questioning of the whereabouts of my family stirred my father into alarming bouts of rage because I refused to believe the lies that he told.

Eventually, after being sick of my crying and questioning, he took me to a grave site and told me that my entire family was dead. Tombstone by tombstone he named them and pointed, daring me to ever ask again. Though I do not remember much of my time in Mexico, one of my memories is picking up the phone and just dialing random numbers saying that I was calling home.

I did this as the years went on until the harsh reality sank in that my family was nowhere to be found. I remember being mad because they never called me. Never came for me. I was exposed to many things while there. Of course, I learned the language of that country. I was fluent in Spanish and spoke broken English. I became my father's translator when at the markets and such.

I was exposed to perversion, drugs, alcohol, lying and violence before the age of five. I saw him snorting cocaine and watching pornographic movies with his friends. I was taken into bars with him. Sometimes I would go to the back where the owner's kids would spend time together and play. These little boys never really knew how to play well with me since they experimented on me with their sexual desires. I remember always being afraid.

Being heavily intoxicated and constantly under the influence, he possessed a rage that came from somewhere much deeper and darker than a human could project. There are just a few memories that I have. I remember collecting tadpoles and crying when I had to let them go because they were getting too big. I remember being a cunning crafty little thing. I racked up a tab at a peanut stand that I passed every day on my two-way commute to the Catholic school I attended.

I always promised to pay but never did. Then that one day, dad walked by with me and found out (because the gentleman chased him down to collect his money). Instead of getting upset, he paid and said, "How in the world did you talk that man into doing that at such a young age? That is my little girl."

I remember laying in the bed one night trembling with fear as my father was under the influence. I remember him coming in the bed with me... then the memory stops.

I remember firing my babysitter because she made me eat guacamole and my father allowed it. I remember trying beer and trying to light cigarettes while my father was passed out. I remember hiding from him at the neighbors, but he would always come and get me. Everyone was afraid of him; no one stopped him. But I remember this day the most. My last day in Mexico. I was 5 years old.

# Chapter 3
## Found

*It's impossible to disappear from you or to ask the darkness to hide me, for your presence is everywhere, bringing light into my night.*

**Psalms 139:11 TPT**

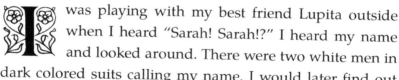 was playing with my best friend Lupita outside when I heard "Sarah! Sarah!?" I heard my name and looked around. There were two white men in dark colored suits calling my name. I would later find out they were FBI agents. As soon as they confirmed my identity, they motioned for other people to come around the corner.

I saw a huge white afro hair first. I knew that white afro in an instant. It was my momaw! 'Momaw' is what we call our grandmothers in the country. I ran and jumped into her arms as I hugged her ever so tight. I then saw the other person coming around the houses. Blonde hair and big bangs; it was my mom! I jumped over momaw's head into my mother's arms. I began to touch and pat her face and say, "Mommy you no dead! I knew you no dead."

They rushed us and allowed me to grab anything I wanted to take quickly. I remember grabbing my favorite doll. It was an old handmade homely looking doll. She was made with cloth and wore a bright colorful dress with yarn for hair. We rushed out of there and was on our way to take the many flights that were ahead.

I was found because my mother had done a news article with Woman's World magazine. A woman in Mexico read the article and called. My father was arrested but he was only detained for a short while— 24 hours. The laws are different in Mexico. I am not sure of all the details but that is what I was told.

We were on a plane to America. My life was changed in an instant. I told jokes and tales the whole time to those agents (whoever they were) and had them laughing the whole time. They could understand Spanish. Mom and momaw just smiled as they could not. That did not matter. Everyone was happy. A miracle had taken place.

# Chapter 4
## Traumatized

*Give all your worries and cares to God, for he cares about you.*

**1 Peter 5:7 NLT**

M y mind ended up shutting down on me. I did not remember much from Mexico. It is like my mind went into hibernation concerning certain experiences I had and even to this day, it is sleeping. Protection? Trauma? Both?

There were cameras and reporters everywhere lined up as I got off the plane. I skipped down the roped-off aisles smiling the whole way unafraid and loving the attention perhaps! There was the reunion with the rest of my family. Then there were the questions. I did not want to talk about Mexico and quite frankly I did not. "I wanted to be an American," I said. I want to be like my big sister. I refused to maintain and even keep the Spanish language. I picked up English quickly and literally refused to have any life but the American life from that moment on. I learned how to shut down, and to pretend at an incredibly early age. So, as time passed, I transitioned into my new life.

To better explain how my mind had shut down, I feel led to write this portion of my story. I was back in the United States for a little while. There was a couple—a man and a woman—from Mexico who came to visit me at my grandmother's house. I remember this like it was yesterday, as the memories are flowing as I am writing this.

I also remember the conversation that they had with my grandmother as she apologized to them as they expressed their shock. They could not understand why I couldn't remember or identify who they were. This was a couple who claimed that they had me almost every day and that I should have been receptive to their visit and remember who they were. I remember looking them straight in their faces and saying, "No I don't remember you." I really didn't. This is the best way I can explain how my mind closed off at such a young age.

They seemed happy that I was happy dancing and running around the house, but I could also see a sadness in their eyes while they were leaving the house. It expressed the wonder of how a child that they had grown to love so dearly and seemed to know so intimately had forgotten all about them.

At this time, it was my grandparents, mom, sister, and myself living in a house together. I remember them taking me to therapy sessions. I remember going to court against my dad and not wanting to say anything to hurt him. Children are resilient, I still loved my father. I just wanted it all to end and just move forward.

Eventually, it got to the point where they stopped trying to get me to talk about the past because I would not. They stopped trying to get me to speak Spanish because I refused. Life began to move ahead.

# Chapter 5
## Uprooted

*And we know that God causes everything to work together for the good of those who love God and are called according to his purpose for them.*

**Romans 8:28 NLT**

WITHIN a few years of being home, my mother decided to take me to Florida. I did not know at that point that she was paranoid schizophrenic. I did not know that she was involved in the drug usage as my father—which I am sure worsened her state of mind.

I was too small to remember what my sister saw them do together. I did not know that my mother had two nervous breakdowns while I was missing and that it had affected her mental health ever more adversely. I did not know that my father had traumatized and abused them to an alarming extent. I did not know what I was in for because of her state of mind.

I remember that day like it was yesterday; a small car loaded with everything she could fit. I remember kicking, screaming, and begging not to leave. I remember jumping in the back seat of that loaded car and finding a hole in the back window to put my face in to see my grandparents begging her not to take off with me.

I remember my last momentary years of a normal safe life with my grandparents and big sister. The next chapter of my life was loading, and the years ahead would break me and send me to places I never thought possible. I was now in the care of an unmedicated, paranoid schizophrenic single parent.

Without the constant chatter of a full house and the distraction of remarkable grandparents and a big sister to annoy, I finally saw that there was something seriously wrong with my mother. I observed irregularities in her personality that made me uncomfortable but never *really* noticed before—now it was front and center with no other distractions. My dear mother, heard voices and saw things—delusions. I became the scapegoat of her illness. I did not know about the spiritual aspect of life then. These voices and visions were very real to her.

# Chapter 6
## New Reality

*For God hath not given us the spirit of fear; but of power,*
*and of love, and of a sound mind.*

### 2 Timothy 1:7 KJV

M y mother dated a family law attorney that loved her more than life itself. He did anything she asked him to do. He satisfied her biddings to the point that it harmed me in the process. It was not too long after, that I started crying out for help to my grandparents. They always had their hands tied because of who was helping my mom.

I endured endless torture for the years ahead. Non-stop screaming day and night to the people she saw who I could not see and the endless conversations with people she could hear that I could not hear. Countless nights, I was awakened to tales of alien abduction and her trying to convince me that I was being taken along with them and experienced the same things she did, such as scientific experiments and being forced to have sexual encounters with these aliens. She always believed she was being followed and stalked and of course I knew about it. I was accused of helping them find her.

Her photos that she had developed were always tampered with and now we had to go on the run because the government was after her. She claimed that we had been kidnapped and the government performed surgery on us implanting microchips in our brains through our noses and they were controlling and monitoring us.

She dated the President some days. If you can think of it, she said it, and sadly believed it. Whenever we went out, you never knew when she was going to have an episode. This led me to a place of always being on the defense, ready at any moment for her to lose control and embarrass me in public.

I couldn't tell you the many places that we've been asked to leave because of her outburst. I could not tell you the many places that we went where she would start screaming for no apparent reason. I couldn't begin to explain the embarrassment and the fear I had of going into public places because of her condition. I never realize until I was older that this part of my life is what brought on so much anxiety of public places to me.

My mother was obsessed with her weight and looks. There was never any food in the house. Her reasoning was that that is how she stayed skinny because she afforded anything else she wanted. I remember calling my grandmother one day and telling her how hungry I was. She told me to open the refrigerator. She asked me what was inside, and I replied "ketchup". That day I learned how to make tomato soup with ketchup, water, salt and pepper. A miracle happened that day to me. I thought I had the coolest grandma around.

My mother would walk around in a daze sometimes. It would be the opposite of her louder screaming matches. She would walk around completely unclothed as if she was there but not there. I would scream her name and there was no response at all. She would just stand there sometimes for a while and then walk away like a robot.

I remember always being deathly afraid of the dark. I know some say that that's normal for a young child, but I would beg to differ. This was a much more deeply rooted fear upon recollection of these memories. I always felt a dark evil presence of someone in my room with me. Someone watching and observing—spying and waiting. There was. I do not want to keep going on. I just want to give you a modest description of the insane asylum where I was imprisoned.

I was afraid of my mother to the point that when we lived in a place that I could lock my door, I did. I slept sometimes with a knife under my pillow. This was my life while going to school and trying to function as a normal child then teen. I had tested for gifted classes, passed well above average to a genius level. I had a chance at doing something well for myself in that aspect, but I could not learn how to function under all this trauma every day.

# Chapter 7
## Destructive Impact

*For we are God's masterpiece. He has created us anew in Christ Jesus, so we can do the good things he planned for us long ago.*

**Ephesians 2:10 NLT**

O N top of my mother's delusions and fantasy worlds, she was very promiscuous. She had any man that would take her. She would bring them home—door shut, door open it did not matter.

Sometimes I saw it—I always had to hear it. She would even take me to the homes of the men she saw. I would have to sit outside their room quietly and not be in the way of their excursions. Of course, I was always told that I was to stay silent and stay out of the way. For years this is what I dealt with on a constant basis.

I was depressed, oppressed, aloof and felt out of place every day and everywhere I went. Many days she would turn on me with her anger and rage. Sometimes she would lock herself up for days at a time in her room to have yelling matches to these unseen people. I would beg her to just come out and be with me. I was always alone. I was not allowed to really do anything unless it was with her or whoever she was seeing. Imprisoned in my own silence.

So, when my grades started slipping and I did not care to do my work anymore, of course I was called every name in the book and chided that there was no reason I should not be performing at a straight A level. She spoke to me in a manner that was not suitable for an animal. I was called ugly, stupid, worthless, useless—you name it! And I claimed it. Let me not forget that she chided me on a regular basis that I would be just like my father. I felt hopeless. I was voiceless. I could not catch a breath. I was bound in torturous silence.

# Chapter 8
## *False Shelter*

*There is a path before each person that seems right, but it ends in death.*

**Proverbs 14:12 NLT**

I always called my grandparents after my choir performances. I went over to the payphone as usual and dialed their phone number (it was the same since I was born) and my grandma answered the phone.

I could hear the sadness in her voice as she asked to speak with my mother. That was the day that we were informed that my grandpa wasn't given a long time to live. I begged my mother that day to let me spend that day with my friends to be comforted. That day she gave in and that was the first day that I got high and drunk.

I was so messed up from drinking that I blacked out and threw up. It was a few hours before I recuperated enough to go home. But before I got sick and passed out, I remember laughing so much and the emotional distress was numbed for that moment. At this time too, I found out that I liked attention from boys; I believe I was starting to really find other ways to receive attention.

I was not even a teenager yet. I thought I finally found my hiding place and shelter from the storms of my life. It brought to me what I had been so desperately desiring. I thought I had found my relief and rescue. I found a way of escape. The only comfort I had found all these years. Little did I know that this was the starting point of a very disastrous journey. I began walking down a path of destruction blindly seeking false refuge. The hate and depression inside me began to boil over.

# Chapter 9
# Orphan

*Father to the fatherless, defender of widows— this is God, whose dwelling is holy.*

**Psalms 68:5 NLT**

My father had been diagnosed with the rarest form of bone cancer. He had gotten the courage to call my grandparent's house. He had been warned previously that if he ever stepped foot on the property, my grandfather would shoot him. However, they were moved with compassion with his distress call, and they allowed him to visit this time.

He came to their house bound to morphine drip—barely able to walk. He knew he was dying and wanted to ask for forgiveness. My mother was called; she didn't want me to see him, but I told her that he was my father and that I wanted to see him. I saw a possible way out.

There were so many questions that I never got to ask him before he died. I was given an opportunity to reconcile with him two weeks before he passed, but I was only 12 years old.

I was young and could not grasp his imminent death due to the severity of the bone cancer that attacked his body. Just being in his presence after all the years of being absent from him and looking upon him in his condition was hard enough to bear. Too much to process and accept. I just sat there staring at his face and then looking at my own to see the resemblance.

When we received the call that he had passed, I remember falling to the floor in the kitchen. Something inside me broke. Despite the childhood pain, I was now an orphan in my mind. I had no hope for rescue. Even while he lived, I felt like an orphan. Therefore, his death verified I was always alone and would always be alone. I was never the same from that day on. I had a false sense of hope and nurtured a possibility of being rescued from my mom, only to be disappointed again.

# Chapter 10
## The Rebellion

*For the world offers only a craving for physical pleasure, a craving for everything we see, and pride in our achievements and possessions. These are not from the Father, but are from this world.*

**1 John 2:16 NLT**

I entered a sphere of full-blown rebellion. I began vocalizing the hatred I felt and protested in every way possible. I hated life, myself and I especially hated my mother. I started to run away. Everything that I once hated I became. I was fighting generational curses I knew nothing of. I tried to find love, comfort, and acceptance from people, paths and substances.

I would leave and stay gone for days sometimes weeks at a time. Partying all the time; living in a state of numbness and staying as far away from home as possible. I did whatever it took to stay away. It did not matter. Young and naive, I never really knew the dangers that were out on the streets. I was willing to take any chance to find or create a new life.

On one occasion, I had run away from home and the police found me. I was hiding in a closet fighting to keep the door closed to stay in that closet. There was a woman officer there. When she saw the fear that gripped me, her countenance changed. She was the first person to ask me what was going on, and why I was afraid to go home. I began to share with her my mother's state of mind and what I had to endure. I was taken to a facility for young people. It was like a safe house for young people while things were getting sorted out.

There was a male worker there (I will call him Mr. D), that I really got close to. I developed a harmless crush for him. There was an incident in the house one day, where one of the youths became violent and began to punch holes in their room. They were strict on male workers being alone with female youths, but this incident caused much confusion that day. It was the first time I was left alone with him in a room. He took full advantage of that time to make me aware he was conscious of my beauty and that he found me very attractive. I was being discharged from the facility and he knew the date. He reached over quickly, brushing over my breast and remarked that he would like to meet up with me when I got out and that he found me very captivating.

As the commotion began to abate, people began to come into the room that we were in. He walked away nonchalantly. I told a girlfriend of mine who was in there with me what had happened. She went on to relate the incident to other workers.

The next day, I was asked to tell my side of the story. I was called into the office and there was one male and a female worker. I will share more about this male worker that was in the room that I had to tell my side of the story to, he too was perverted but I would not know this until later. The person that I ran away from—my mother— was then contacted. I was taken into a small white room with a camera and then videotaped as I gave my testimony.

The outcome was that they believed his story over mine. I was asked to leave the facility as they did not believe my side of the incident. They called for my mother to come get me negating the help I desperately needed. I was banned from even coming on the property. I was finally speaking, only to be silenced in turn. The rejection of receiving real help and the reality that the little hope that I had was taken away, began to take root. I lost hope and respect for authority. The lie of only being worth my body was reinforced.

I realized once again that if anyone was going to help me, it was going to be me, along the path that I would make for myself. I truly believed at this point that there was no real help. I was willing to take any chance possible at a different life at any cost and I determined that I would just keep trying. Eventually, I would find someone safe and someone to love me.

# Chapter 11
## Dangers Lurking

*The thief's purpose is to steal and kill and destroy.*
*My purpose is to give them a rich and satisfying life.*

**John 10:10 NLT**

 feel lead to share this portion of my story, I have not thought about this once in all the years that have passed.

I had a neighbor when we lived in an apartment complex. This guy lived about two apartment buildings down in front of me. My friends and I were always hanging outside and he always creeped me out whenever I saw him. We asked him once to buy us some cigarettes and alcohol to drink. He obliged. I could tell that he had ulterior motives. I mean, what grown man would buy underage girl's alcohol? He went to the store and got them for us but when he came back, he went straight into his apartment. He did this so that we would have to come up to his place to get them.

We were scared, but we walked up there together and decided that we would not go inside. I stood by the steps while she knocked. He opened the door and asked her in. She told him no and explained to him that we just wanted what he went to the store to get.

He went inside to get the alcohol and returned while standing inside out of my friend's reach. She walked in halfway and tried to snatch it from him. He held on and tried to shut her inside. As she tried to make her way out, he grabbed her hand then notice that I was there as well. We made a dash for it. She said that when she looked around inside his loft apartment, she noticed that he had these black curtains hung up to hide the loft area upstairs. She said that she had the eeriest feeling that we were to never speak to him again.

I noticed that whenever I went out to different places, I would see his car. He had an older car that no one drove; it was a car that stood out like a sore thumb. I started to get the sense that he was following me. Nothing came of it because I became aware of my surroundings, but I felt very strongly that he had seriously evil intentions.

I was extremely happy when we moved away, especially for the fact that my mother's episodes could not be hidden or ignored when living in close quarters with other residents. Of course, we never told anyone of the incident, but I feel like this needs to be shared for a reason.

# Chapter 12
# Captive

*The Spirit of the Sovereign Lord is upon me, for the Lord has anointed me to bring good news to the poor. He has sent me to comfort the brokenhearted and to proclaim that captives will be released and prisoners will be freed.*

*Isaiah 61:1 NLT*

A<small>T</small> the age of 14, I was introduced to a man and his girlfriend who offered me a way out. Two days after 9-11, I arrived in NY on a grey hound bus. I could smell the smoke and death and see the destruction and devastation. We immediately took a taxi to New Jersey. I was about to be awakened to the reality I found myself in that same day. We all had fake IDs made, new name, age, address. Again, a false identity.

I stood outside of the strip club and just stared at it. I began to feel the fear of where I was and what I was about to do. I did not want to go forward with it. I decided that I had jumped in too deep. It was too late however to turn back.

I voiced my fear to this guy who I thought was my friend.

I was unknowingly in the clutches of a pimp. I did not even know what a pimp was or that they existed. The abuse began immediately—although it had already begun—I just did not understand it as abuse. He had begun grooming me in Florida.

I was rapped and threatened almost every day by him. He embedded in me the things he would do to me if I did not listen to him. He did and said whatever it took to keep control of me. He told me stories of what he had done to other women that did not listen and obey him. He graphically explained raping women with a broomstick and other objects and the injuries they sustained. Story after story was laid on me like butter on a bread. So much terror gripped me. I was afraid to speak, I was terrified to run.

I was forced to dance and sell myself against my will. The life that I now lived, I could not manage sober. What was required of me— the pieces of me that were being given and taken away—I had to delve deeper into drugs. I began taking the drug ecstasy and drinking heavier than ever. This is how I could numb my mind so that I could listen and obey him with the least number of consequences (although no matter what, there was some sort of violence and abuse).

I endured this agonizing life day after day. One day seemed like a year. I was exhausted; bound in my mind, emotions, and body. My only escape was in a drink or drug. I never slept. I was always afraid as I was constantly monitored and controlled.

# Chapter 13
## Lethal

*"But I came by and saw you there, helplessly kicking about in your own blood. As you lay there, I said, 'Live!'*

**Ezekiel 16:6 NLT**

I was working one night in one of the clubs as I always did. It was a full nude strip club with no rules or limitations. This particular club was where the gang known as the 'Bloods' hung out. I was sitting in the dressing room. I do not know how long I was sitting there, lost in an emotionless stare.

A group of the dancers came up to me and began talking to me. They were 'Bloodettes' and they wanted to befriend me. They said they had been watching me and noticed that "that man" was always here with me. They did not like what they saw and said that I could come with them and get away from his grip. They could tell that I was young and completely captive. I do not know how long it took me to respond, but I numbingly shook my head "yes". Then paralyzing fear instantly arose inside of me. I knew that I had to act quickly. I began to get dressed.

I do not know how he found out I was leaving, but he did. I was getting dressed behind a locked bathroom door when he came rushing in knocking his way through the door as I was sitting on the toilet rushing to get my other shoe on. He came in with such force breaking through the locked door tackling me, breaking the tank of the commode with my back. He grabbed me by my throat with one hand and began to punch me mercilessly and repeatedly in the face.

He carried me through the club while beating me the whole way out. I was spitting out chunks of flesh and choking on my own blood. The girls ran behind us screaming for him to let me go.

He motioned for a taxi and threw me in the back of it. He took off his smooth black leather jacket my money had bought him and threw it on top of me. He told the driver to take us back to our hotel room. On arrival at the hotel, he dragged me out of the car, dragged me up the stairs and threw me inside the cold, dark, run-down hotel room. I just knew that this was my final moments alive. Though I despaired life, I could not believe these were my final moments; this was how my life was going to end.

He began slapping and biting me, he was exhausted from beating me. He didn't have the energy to keep punching me. He rebuked me for bleeding on him, he was enraged that my blood covered him. "How dare you bleed on me" are the last words I remember before he threw my lifeless body in the shower and turned on the water. He further demanded that I stopped bleeding and get cleaned up. I just laid there unable to move, water beating down on me. I could barely see, but I could faintly make out the outline of his figure as his fist drew back for one more punch, then it was as if something or someone unseen stopped him in mid strike. He stood there motionless and in what appeared like paralysis and confusion, he pulled back and dropped his fist, turned around and walked away.

I was beaten so badly that he hid me out for weeks at his friend's apartment. People were stopping and staring at me and asking me who had done that to me. Complete strangers would ask if they could help me. I could not even hold my head up or look anyone in the eye. I looked deformed from the beating, unable to see or speak clearly. With my abuser staying closely to me, I would walk forward and ignore the questions. He was afraid I would speak so he decided he would wait until I looked somewhat normal to allow me to be seen in public.

I was unable to eat or speak for weeks. I only drank from a straw. He would mock me and laugh at me stating he was sure I learned my lesson. Eventually I had healed enough to get back to work as he said. He would just take me to another club. So back to it I went. Day after day, week after week. I finally decided I did not care what happened; I was going to get away. I ran into someone I had met before. There were people from the previous club looking for me. He got someone to distract him, and we just ran for it.

I was finally free from this tyrant, only to stay under the rulership of the streets. I still had to survive on the streets as a runaway teenager.

# Chapter 14
# Confrontation

*Dear friends, never take revenge. Leave that to the righteous anger of God. For the Scriptures say, "I will take revenge; I will pay them back," says the Lord.*

*Romans 12:19 NLT*

ONE night, I walked into the same club that I was almost beaten half to death in. I had not been back to that club since that night. Upon entering, I started to violently shake in terror. The Bloodettes that I was now living with all started crying with me as I was frozen in fear after the report came to me that my old pimp was inside. This time I had the whole gang backing me, but this meant nothing as I was deathly afraid of my ex-abuser.

One of the male Bloods came up to me and he looked me square in the eye and placed a gun in my hands and spoke these words: "There are never witnesses here. We do not see or speak about anything. We all have your back no harm will come to you tonight."

I walked into that club with a gun in my pants shaking all

over. When he saw me, and I saw him, we locked eyes and he began to make his way towards me until he saw everyone walking around me. He fell back and just watched with a confused expression. I could see the rage mixed with fear in his eyes. For once he couldn't touch me.

I sat at the bar and ordered a drink trying to stop the involuntary trembling in my entire body. You could sense the heightened tension and smell the emotion in the air. I could almost taste revenge. I drank the drink and ordered another. I sat there staring at him with intense hatred. I thought of every touch, every word, every rape, every experience I had endured with him.

I wanted him to die. But a quick death didn't seem like a just punishment for the likes of him. I pulled out the gun that I had tucked in my pants and rested in on my lap under the bar table. I looked around and saw that my tribe was around me in full defense waiting to pounce if necessary. They had watchful eyes on him. Their gaze went back and forth from him to me. They were waiting for me to make my move; waiting for the sound of shots fired. There were whispers along with their stares. The only thought in my mind in that moment was whether I wanted to spend the rest of my life behind bars. I wrestled with that thought. In that moment, that was the only thought that kept me from pulling the trigger.

I had another drink. With tears flowing down my cheeks, I tucked the gun back in my pants and walked up to the guy who gave it to me. I was still violently shaking. He looked at me with such compassion in his eyes; a man who probably had only known violence and street life. He took the gun and stared at me some more. His eyes penetrated my tired, sad soul. There was an unspoken conversation in that moment. It was like he said, "You are safe now, you do not have to go through with it."

They escorted me out of the club. I was inside their 'safety circle'. I heard a ruckus behind me. He wanted to grab a hold of me so badly I could see it. I left that night and never went back to that place.

# Chapter 15
## Tainted

*"Are you weary, carrying a heavy burden? Come to me. I will refresh your life, for I am your oasis. Simply join your life with mine. Learn my ways and you'll discover that I'm gentle, humble, easy to please. You will find refreshment and rest in me.*

*Matthew 11:28-29 TPT*

I had been exposed to so many things up to this point in my life. Drugs of many descriptions and every form of sexual perversion. I did not find what I was looking for. I found more pain, bondage, and sorrow. Even the pleasures I tried to find were fleeting. None of it filled the empty places in my soul. Trying to fill the emptiness inside only created a deeper void. Every well I had drunk from only made me thirstier. Every table I sat at dished me bowls of toxins that poisoned my soul.

# Weathered

*It began as a quiet storm.*

*Sprinkles of soft sky waters began to transform.*

*Soft winds began spiking, starting to reform.*

*Locked in a vault of torturous silence,*

*Raging gusts thrusting my balance.*

*Agony latched on like a fisherman's hook,*

*Laments from the black keys written in my songbook.*

*I must elude this place where chains adorn,*

*Barley alive, resisting blatant scorn.*

*This disaster sped faster,*

*Bondage my master,*

*False escape left a bitter taste.*

*The perfect storm, many don't survive face to face.*

# Chapter 16
## Next Move

*Brush off the dust and get to your feet, captive Jerusalem!*
*Throw off your chains, captive daughter of Zion!*

### Isaiah 52:2 MSG

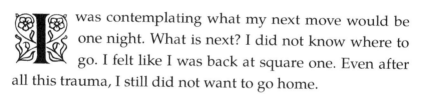 was contemplating what my next move would be one night. What is next? I did not know where to go. I felt like I was back at square one. Even after all this trauma, I still did not want to go home.

I remember this night vividly. I was at the club dancing, as usual. I had not slept in three nights because I was consuming too much ecstasy nightly so that I could "perform". I only had the courage and confidence under the influence. My attire that night was chains. I wore a metal meshed chain linked dress that fell all the way down to the ground as if it was a gown. It was the embodiment of bondage from the inside out.

I had just taken another ecstasy pill before I came out. They announced my stage name over the speaker. Three, two, one…show time! The stage was in the center of the square-shaped bar tabletop. Often, we would move from the stage to the bar tabletop where the gentlemen would sit and drink if they showed interest and the money was right. We had many there that were regulars. We knew them by name, we knew what they were about. Ever so often, they wanted conversation because they were lonely.

Tonight, there were two handsome men that stood out from the rest. I had never seen them before. I noticed that the other women were trying to get their attention but to no avail. For some reason, they were locked in on me. Of course, I knew that is where my attention needed to go as they were intent on showing their interest in me. I thought to myself, *at least they are good looking so it would not be so hard tonight to entertain them.* I moved closer to them. I could not identify what I was feeling as I got closer.

The moment I locked eyes with them, it was like a chill went through me and a fogginess lifted. I could see clearly in their eyes, and they were reading deeply into mine. They carried some sort of authority with them, and I could sense it. A realization came over me; I was aware of my nakedness. I felt the shame of being naked. They asked me my name and of course I gave them my alias. They then asked me to sit down and have a conversation with them. I obliged. That is usually the protocol anyway.

We began conversating. They wanted to know who I was, where I was from, how old I was and why I was in a place like this. I retorted with, "Why are you in a place like this asking me all these questions." They just sat there looking me up and down as if they had no answer. Finally, the silence broke. They proceeded to explain that whenever they went out it was not usually to places like this, but for some reason they were here tonight.

This was not the usual place to hang out, especially on this side of town —a gang infested strip club. But tonight, here they were and here I was. They emphasized how they were by no means perfect men, but they could not figure out what led them to this club. I of course did not know what to say. It was awkward and I was at a loss for words. I sat there for a moment in the awkwardness and palpable silence. I felt a sense of safety for a moment then shook it off. Some part of me was saying, "Introduce yourself, the real you, your real name".

Their gaze never shifted from me. They looked at me intently the entire time. It was as if they relished in the moment. They reintroduced themselves to me. One was an officer of the law, and the other was a correctional officer. I do not know how long we sat and talked. The conversation was geared mostly towards how I was too beautiful to be living this kind of life.

They both agreed that they believed that I was too young to even be in a place like this. Every comment they made was to reassure me that I was in the wrong place and that I needed to make a change. One of them grabbed my face and just held it. Staring with a deep gaze, he asked me if I was tired. He said, "You have the face of an angel". Somehow still, he could see my innocence. I thought to myself, *how could this be?* He said even in the darkness of the room, he could see the dark circles under my eyes. I looked worn and weak.

I wanted to run away. I could not understand all the emotions running through me. I did not think they would still be there when I came back out. I went into the privacy of the changing area and sat there, trying to grasp what just took place.

I decided to go back out. They had taken much of my time, and I had not made the money I needed for the night. So, I went back out with my game face on, expecting them to be gone. To my surprise, they were sitting there waiting for me. As I came back out, they motioned me over. Immediately they asked me if I wanted help. They discussed it between themselves and agreed that they wanted to help me. They did not know what and all I would need help with, but they were sure they were here on this night for me.

They did not know many things, but one thing they were certain of, was that I needed to leave this place. I was somewhere I did not belong and that was evident to them. I told them that I did not know them, but yes, I wanted something different. I wondered in my mind; how could I know they were not going to harm me more than I already had been? Then something inside me said GO. I looked up at them and a trust came over me. I said "OK" and got the one outfit I had with me, changed, and followed them out wondering, *what in the world am I doing*? I was exhausted. I honestly didn't have the strength or the mental capacity to keep doing what I was doing.

# Chapter 17
## What's Next

*You can make many plans, but the Lord's purpose will prevail.*

**Proverbs 19:21 NLT**

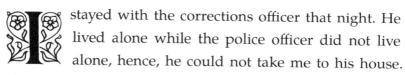stayed with the corrections officer that night. He lived alone while the police officer did not live alone, hence, he could not take me to his house. The next day I awoke sober. Fear gripped me. What was next and where am I? What was I doing?

That next day, the police officer came over to check on me and said that he was taking me clothes shopping. I didn't need to go back where I had previously been to get anything. He wanted me to be dressed as I should and that was as a beautiful, modest young lady. He took me to an expensive store and helped me pick out nice clothes. He made sure that I had underwear, bras, shoes, everything. When we were done, he just looked at me and smiled and told me how stunning I looked covered up. I chose to wear a long-fitted sweater dress that he had picked out and just purchased. We went to grab some take out then drove and parked near the bridge by the water and had conversation.

He began to tell me more about himself and how he liked to take photographs as a hobby. He pulled out his camera and began to recollect the day of 9-11, where he was and how he was driving when it happened. He related how he was able to take pictures of the attack on the world trade center. He showed me pictures he had taken of the explosion. He was able to take shots of it happening in real time. The airplane in mid-air, pictures of the planes crashing into the buildings and the explosion as it was happening.

What he showed me was somber. He expressed his guilt yet relief that he was not around when it happened. I just sat there and listened intently, mostly trying to figure out why I was sitting here with this gentleman I met in a strip club listening to him bare his heart to me. I patiently listened as he took breaks, he continued his account of the story. He would stop momentarily to stare at me and then he would go on.

He then shifted the conversation and tried to get me to talk about me. It did not work. I was like a locked vault. I knew I was an underage run- away living a lie. All I would say is that I had a bad home life and that as soon as I was 18, I left home and here is where I had found myself. He made it noticeably clear he did not believe. He said he would give me some time but eventually I would have to come clean. He did not pressure me anymore. He took me back to his friend's house as he was about to go on shift.

The same questioning came from the other guy. Again, I gave the same answer. He as well made it clear that he did not believe me. He backed off as well that day. He worked 12-hour shifts, so I began to spend more time alone—sober—with my thoughts and the residuals of trauma. I did not know how to manage that.

He was the first person ever to sit down with me and tell me to write my story. He obviously knew that I had much to share. As time went on, the pressure for honesty came and I was not ready to divulge. He had a friend of his who came over one day. When he noticed that I was there alone, he started to come over increasingly when he was at work. I was extremely uncomfortable. He then started to make his move. I made it crystal clear that I was not interested in him.

There were several instances where I had to push him off me and get away. I did not know what to say. I did not want to cause any problems between him and his friend. I thought I had found a break but, I was right back at square one. The pressure between having to tell the truth and then this guy trying to force himself on me after I finally thought I had a choice was too much. I decided to go to a club again. If I was going to have to endure that kind of pressure once more, I would decide which of the evils was better.

# Chapter 18
## Another Move

*Let me hear of your unfailing love each morning, for I am trusting you. Show me where to walk, for I give myself to you.*

**Psalms 143:8 NLT**

I went to a strip club one night and did as I had decided— not forced or for free. I knew my time of safety was up and I would have to make my own money and figure out my next move. I sat at the bar and had a few drinks. I changed my mind about dancing. I didn't have the willpower anymore. I decided I was just going to tip the girls, drink and have a night out.

After a few drinks, I was lit because I had not been drinking for a while. A guy and his friend came into the club, and he stood close to me. We hit it off and started talking and laughing. One thing led to the other and we left together and spent the night together.

He dropped me off the next morning and I snuck into the correctional officer's house. I was questioned about my whereabouts and the whole nine. I finally talked about his friend and how he had been behaving towards me. I was angry that I had to be left alone in that situation with someone he said he trusted. I did not stay long after that.

I ended up dating the guy I met in the club. I lived with his mom for a while then I lived with him. We loved each other the best way we knew how. We had our difficulties. He did not like me drinking or smoking—he was intent on that.

He was young and living the life of a hustler which was all he knew then. Our paths were crossed just for a little while. It just was not meant to be. I eventually went home to Florida. I was honest with him about my age and situation and with some issues that arose between us, I left the same way I had come—on a greyhound bus with a one-way ticket.

Our departure from one another was heart rending. We genuinely cared for each other, but it was time to say goodbye. It was a season and it had ended. The next chapters of our lives were starting. I was going back where I came from, more broken than when I had left. I was full of secrets and shame. I vowed to never speak of what happened. Silence.

# Chapter 19
## *Misunderstood*

*For I can do everything through Christ, who gives me strength.*

**Philippians 4:13 NLT**

I called my mom from the bus station in Florida when I arrived. She came and picked me up. She did not believe that I was really where I said I was. Yet, there I sat waiting when she came. I was angry that I was there—back to where I wanted to be away from. But I was tired of running. I was oh so tired.

I WAS AN ECHO OF WHAT I WAS EXPOSED TO ALL MY LIFE. I had become a monster. Cruel. Bitter. Hateful. Enraged.

I would not listen to anyone for any reason. Like the saying goes, "hurt people hurt people". I was beyond hurt! Hurt is not the adjective I really want to use. I was harmed so I didn't care who I harmed. I bled on people who didn't cut me. I was injured internally and externally, and I didn't think there was any help for me.

The example that my mother gave me was that you don't receive help mentally or emotionally. She refused to get the help that she needed, so I didn't understand that there was healing or help for the mind or for emotions. I didn't know how I would deal with these issues, so I coped the best way, the only way I had ever known. That way was to stay under the shelter, the only shelter that was always there and that is suppression in any form.

No one could understand what was wrong with me. No one could understand the hell that I had been through my whole life—the hell that I had found trying to make a way for myself. No one knew or truly understood. All they saw was the outside rebellious young girl. No one understood or saw the wounded little girl that had never really had safety or stability. People had lots of opinions, but no one knew the truth. I couldn't understand myself. I didn't comprehend the violence and abuse I found myself in at every turn I made. Pain and sorrow had become my portion and it was all I ever knew. I trusted no one; not even myself.

# Chapter 20
## Predators

*So then, surrender to God. Stand up to the devil and resist him and he will flee in agony.*

*James (Jacob) 4:7 TPT*

I argued and fought now with my mother more than ever. I never held back my hate for her and her illness that I did not understand. I blamed her for everything I went through. I was captive at home and everywhere I tried to escape. I skipped school and did the exact opposite of what was right.

I did not care about myself or life. I was reckless. I was violent. I was as sick as my secrets. I did whatever it took to get what I wanted. I didn't know a day of peace. I didn't know a day of love. The law ended up knowing me by name. I was always in some sort of fight or trouble. I wound up on probation for getting into some trouble.

This is where I want to share about that other man in the room at the youth facility that I had to tell my side of the story to. He was one of the correctional officers that worked at the Juvenile Detention Center I wounded up in for a short while. I remember walking into a room in the detention center and there he stood. Of course, I remembered him, and he remembered me.

He smiled with an extra big grin and began to make conversation. I did not know that he was even more perverted than the other man at the other facility. All I knew of him was that he was one of the workers at the other facility that had to take my side of the story when the worker had approached me the way that he did. He never came on to me at the other place. He did not bother me in any inappropriate way while I was in the detention center either, it was only upon my release.

There are a lot of predators that take jobs and positions of authority or leadership in pretentions of helping when they are seeking their meal to fill their desires—hunting easy prey. The young people that are in their care and association are very vulnerable and very impressionable and they take advantage of them. There are a lot of young people who needed an escape from abuse or neglect or whatever their case may be only to walk into these predator's trap. There are wolves in sheep's clothing everywhere and from my experiences they work together knowingly or unknowingly.

Some of the girls at the facility made comments that he was a pervert. It is not that I did not believe them, I just knew he had never approached me that way. I never gave it a second thought. He was always nice to me and made me laugh. Besides, he was one of the workers that took my side of the story before when the sexual advances were made towards me. He was not like most of the workers there; he was different. He liked to make you feel comfortable and always kept a smile on your face. Very welcoming and enticing these types of people are.

When I was released to do my probation, the calls started to come to my house. Yes, he began to call my home phone number. He had gotten my information from my file. He had my phone number and home address. I remember hanging the phone up and a chill went down my spine. The calls persisted. I would hang up on him every time he called.

I noticed this small old beaten-up car driving past my house at a slow crawl. I ran outside trying to see inside the car one day. I wanted to see if the driver was someone I knew. It was him. He was stalking my house. One day he called, and I answered. He asked (as he always did) for me to meet up with him. I was a little brave that day and wanted to see how far this guy was willing to go (I do not recommend this to anyone).

He told me where he would meet me which was at the park in my neighborhood. He had seriously canvassed my neighborhood. He gave me a time and date to meet him. I remember walking to the park that day, I was terrified, but I thought that maybe if I told him in person to stop stalking me, that he would. I hit the corner of the park and saw the old small car sitting, waiting. Something in me said *turn back. This is not a way to make your point.* That was one time I can say fear led me to turn back to a place of safety. I never told anyone. Who was there to tell? I figured it was pointless. No-one listened to me before. Why would I put myself in an embarrassment position again? I did not trust authorities even more; these predators, they are everywhere. I just kept it a secret, up until now.

# Chapter 21
# New Drug: Power

*Now my beloved ones, I have saved these most important truths for last: Be supernaturally infused with strength through your life-union with the Lord Jesus. Stand victorious with the force of his explosive power flowing in and through you.*

*Ephesians 6:10 TPT*

I found a new drug and that was POWER. What was once used over me for my body, I now realized I could use it for control over someone else's. I had become addicted to sexual gratification. I had previously discovered pleasure in pain.

I found sex to be meaningless—just a sensual pleasure. Numbed from the exposure of perversion, I saw it as a transactional encounter. Give and take. Failed attempts to share meaning in this intimate experience left me apathetic and detached. I wanted to be in control now, unaffected and numb towards someone professing their affection.

I began snorting cocaine at this point. My house was the party house. It was a constant; it never ceased. Becoming what I hated pierced me deeper than any knife could puncture. Identifying myself as who I was, by what I had done. I despised the lifestyle but didn't know how to change it. I didn't know that there was a way out. I didn't know any other way.

Conditioned through the pressures of my existence in this world that I had been exposed to, I didn't feel worthy of anything good. I didn't know how to love or be loved. I jeered at love's existence.

Name it and claim it. I was everywhere doing everything yet accomplishing nothing all the time. If there was a door that darkness opened, I walked through it. Darkness always beckoned for me, calling me my name. Darkness always made me feel wanted and accepted but it came with a high price.

# Chapter 22
## Desired Death

*And I am convinced that nothing can ever separate us from God's love. Neither death nor life, neither angels nor demons, neither our fears for today nor our worries about tomorrow—not even the powers of hell can separate us from God's love.*

**Romans 8:38 NLT**

THERE were instances where my mother called 911 and the ambulance showed up because she could not wake me up. I had partied too hard the days or nights before. They would come to wake me up and make sure I was alive and that was it. They were like, "Oh, that is just Sarah. She is fine. She just partied too hard as usual."

I was Baker Acted (admitted to a mental health hospital to be mentally assessed) a few times. Once for threatening the police officers because I was already aggravated from being jumped by a few girls that I had almost resorted to knife violence earlier that night. I have had my stomach pumped a few times. Nothing stopped me from my pursuit of the worldly pleasures. I always wanted to die anyway. I pushed everything to the limits.

The assurance of having final peace is what death bargained with me with. Death kept bringing this option to the table. I remember so many nights I would sit down with knives and try to slit my wrists. I would sit for hours trying to convince myself to follow through and just end it. I would sit and practice trying to do it. Little cuts turned into a little deeper cut.

I could not follow through with it. I do like pain unlike many people who have done this. I did not want more pain. For me, I wanted the pain to end. So, after so many years and so many failed attempts with minor cuts, I decided I would try another way.

At this point, I was seeing an ex-NFL player. He was the one who found me. I decided I was going to take a whole bottle of pills and drink a gallon of wine. I remember sitting at the kitchen table and grabbing a pen and paper; I was going to write my goodbye letter. I was woozy and the room started to spin after about two lines and as I looked at the letter it was not legible at all. As the pen went straight down the paper, I fell out of the chair.

My last recollection of that night is this; I managed to roll over on my knees and the last words I screamed out was, "God if you are real help me!" I woke up three days later in my bed with no memory of those three days. My boyfriend was there. He told me that he had taken care of me the whole time.

He saw the empty pill bottle and asked a Pharmacy worker what to do with taking too much of that medicine.

I was so mean at the time. He said he was afraid to take me to the hospital because of how he knew I would react. The reply was that the pill was coated, and it was created in a way that if you took too many, your body would automatically reject it. For three days, I did not eat or drink, but my body rejected it.

He said he picked me up and bathed me and that he tried to get water in me. However, as soon as it would hit my tongue, I would throw up. I was out for three days, and when I finally woke up, I realized that my attempt did not work.

Instead of being thankful, I was angry. I was angry that I was alive, and I began to say and think to myself, *you are such a failure just like they all said. They are right. You can't even kill yourself properly. You are an idiot.*

# Chapter 23
# Racial Tension

*There is no longer Jew or Gentile, slave or free, male and female. For you are all one in Christ Jesus. And now that you belong to Christ, you are the true children of Abraham. You are his heirs, and God's promise to Abraham belongs to you.*

*Galatians 3:28-29 NLT*

I N the areas that I lived in Florida, I was the minority (with regard to ethnicity). I say this as an expression to validate the circumstances, but I never "felt" as if I was a minority. I felt blessed to be surrounded by so much culture.

Having the background already of living in Mexico and now living in the melting pot of the United States, the "Sunshine" State Florida, I adopted and enjoyed the cultures around me. I love all people, all color. The problem was, I was always in the middle of racial wars. I couldn't help what my preferences were as far as dating or who I hung around nor was I apologetic.

I fought tooth and nail with anyone who came against me. I had to defend myself all the way. From peers to family to foes—racism was everywhere. There was always someone around to say something negative whether it was my own "race" as they call it or another. I was told I was too white from some and from others I was told I was too black. I was unapologetically just me. That was then and has always been something. I despise racism.

I had to learn how to fight, not only because of where I had been, but because of where I was now. I've been jumped several times. I couldn't quite understand it, but I held my own. I couldn't understand why I was fighting for skin color purposes to say the least and I seemed to stand somewhere in the middle of this crazy war. People always assumed my ethnicity to be many things, from black and white to Columbian to Latino mixed. I am not sure what ethnicity my parents were, but they both had the appearance of Caucasian.

Now this does not pertain to everyone but I'm just sharing what my experiences were. I was called names from all sides, ridiculed by all sides and argued with all sides of the racism pool; from those that were "my color" and those that were not. The funny thing is I don't even know what I am when people ask me my ethnicity. I've always hated having to check that box of Caucasian or white because who truly is just one of those boxes? I have not fit most boxes I have been placed in all my life anyway.

# Condemning Created Color

Gifted with sight.

Endowed with this magnificent contribution to our senses—

The windows of our soul.

The ability to perceive,

Recognizing breath-taking hues.

Humanity.

What a wonder of color having acquired a Genesis conceived in the imagination of the

Creator of color.

Created colors.

An infinite palette from the artist Yahweh.

Oppressors working through mankind have attempted to mute colors,

Condemning His divine created color.

The human psyche, entombed with a darkened veil of deceit.

Vast amounts of master pieces we call human having endured with extreme fortitude.

What if we would begin lifting the layers adversity and affliction have attributed

By unveiling generational deception.

Grasping this revelation, the origin of created colors conception.

Deception must bow down to the actuality of truths reality.

One simply does not condemn the change of colors separate seasons introduce.

Not one soul stares at the vibrancy of the flowers of the field and rebukes the individuality each of its kind possesses.

The colorful promise in the sky we see after a summers rain doesn't produce disdain from the viewer.

One must begin to wonder why created colors are weaponing one another's diversity though still possessing basic creation uniformly the same.

Does not the Potter have every right to create as it is pleasing to Him?

We gaze upon the very image of the Creator as we observe one another face to face.

*Unveiling this transformational truth is where we commence.*

*Embarking on the truth train bringing all others aboard.*

*Become this living epistle, read of all men.*

*Be resolved in this revelation, today you saw your Creator in the face of another—His created color.*

# Chapter 24
# False Hope

*But those who hope in the Lord will renew their strength.*
*They will soar on wings like eagles; they will run and not*
*grow weary, they will walk and not be faint.*

**Isaiah 40:31 NIV**

I had been pursued by a certain man for several years. I would not give a second thought to him. He just seemed "too nice" and courteous. At this point, I did not want any steadfast or significant relationship. I had tried and failed in this area only to intertwine myself in more abuse. He saw me at my best. He saw me in my worst. Yet he persisted.

Nothing I did or say kept him away. Whether I was dating someone or was single, he would always check up on me. He always showed up. He became a constant. It did not matter the condition I was in; he never stopped pursuing me. See, I had a core belief system in operation that was laced with deception. I did not believe there were good people in the world. I did not believe I was loveable or that honorable love existed. I did not believe I could be loved. Wanted and used yes, but love was never an option for me. Exploitation was my lot and portion.

He was unmovable and unshakeable. So, after years of just allowing him to cater to my needs when I chose, something eventually broke in me. The thought hit me that, *hey this guy is different, he had seen me; all of me, and he never flinched, he wanted me more.* His pursuit finally won.

I felt walls breaking down inside without understanding how. This yearning for a deeper intimacy awakened. I began to allow him to gain access into layers of myself no one had accessed. I began to allow him to come to me as he pleased and when I expected to be disappointed, he always disproved my assumptions. He became trusted. He made it a point to stay in constant contact every day. He brought me breakfast in the morning and dinner at night. He was becoming my best friend just by his kindness, gentleness, and consistency. He allowed me to feel parts of myself come alive.

When hope came alive, love awakened and arose, and faith followed suit. Hope allowed me to see a glimpse of a future I never thought possible. He spoke life into me. He spoke of the light he saw in me. Foolish words they were to me, but I ate it up like honey on a stick. I did not believe what he spoke, but I wanted him to keep spoon feeding me. He was ever so gentle with me—his words, his touch and his gaze.

He proposed to me one day in the kitchen in front of my mother. I remember laughing and telling him to get off the floor. The look on his face was that of pain and rejection.

He was serious and I had just rejected him. He got up and walked out and I was left speechless. The next day, I apologized, but made it clear he did not want to marry "someone" like me. After all, look at who I had become and what I had allowed to shape me.

I ECHOED DARKNESS.

We went on as if nothing ever happened. He kept telling me that he had something to say to me. I never went to his place. I felt like I was in control and safe if I controlled the environment that we were in. We would go out for weekend getaways by the beach. We went out on dates to various places. I never wanted to get in close quarters with his personal life (my choice of course). I figured that was one boundary I could maintain so that when it all came crumbling down it would not be so devastating.

He pulled into my driveway one day and when he came out of the of the vehicle, I noticed immediately that he had all his jewelry on and dressed to the nines. I then observed that he wore a ring on his ring finger. I stared at it as he came walking towards me. My thoughts were everywhere. He asked me to come inside so that we could talk.

As we went inside, he said, "Sarah, I have been wanting to talk to you about something for a while now and you have not really wanted to talk. So, I thought I would show you better than I can just say it." I grabbed his hand immediately and asked him why he had a ring on his finger. He looked deeply at me and said, "I am married."

There was no hesitation in my response. I absolutely lost it. I spoke in rage. I lost my temper and grabbed a crystal ashtray that was in the house. He ran out the front door as I threw it. He slammed the door shut just in the nick of time. It crashed in the front door and broke into a million pieces, just like my heart. I was barefoot and went running through the glass to chase him out of the driveway.

Tears flowing down my face, he tried to get me to calm down as he noticed that my feet were bleeding excessively. I looked down and saw a huge, deep wound on my foot. Blood just poured out like a broken pipe. It did not stop my anger, it only fueled it. I recited the words, "I hate you," over and over. When he tried to get out of the car to come near me, I would scream at him louder. He called an ambulance to come before he left, he knew there was no getting near me at this point.

He left when the ambulance and the police officer came. I was embarrassed, hurt and in much pain as the adrenaline began to wear off.

It just so happened that the police officer that came was one that I knew, and he had a liking for me that he had voiced in the past. He asked me what happened, I shared, then refused to go to the hospital. He asked the ambulance workers for a moment with me. He said that he knew I was upset to the point of not realizing how bad the wound was and that he would accompany me as he knew the wound would require many stiches. I took a deep breath and went. He stayed with me until the doctor was finished stitching my wound and I was released from the Emergency Room.

Within a few days, my "boyfriend" returned, and we talked. He began to explain to me that he was in the middle of a divorce, that his marriage was just a piece of paper and had been for a long time as he knew of her infidelities for a while. He said he was serious about being with me and that they had been separated for quite a while, but the divorce was not finalized. Here I was upset, and I was the other woman! After all the married men my mother had brought in and out of our house, I followed in her footsteps. Who knows how many married men I entertained on the stages I performed? It had all numbed me to this level of degradation.

The moment I had been waiting for had arrived. The disappointment that I had prepared for. I knew better than believing for something good to happen to me. I should have known better. I was so desperate to have something good in my life.

He convinced me to wait it out. He was taking a job far away. When the time came for him to leave for training, he made me promise that I would leave and move to West Virginia to live with my grandmother. He knew if I stayed, it would not work. He feared I would not agree to a life of marriage and commitment. He knew the fears I carried, and he knew I would run.

# Chapter 25
# Empty Promises

*If we are unfaithful, he remains faithful, for he cannot deny who he is.*

**2 Timothy 2:13 NLT**

 made a promise to go when he did. I was ready for a new life of being loved by someone—someone who wanted me for the rest of my life.

I was on a path of searching for love my whole life and this led me to see this as a real possibility even though it was morally wrong. I did not know what morals were at that time. I was barely twenty.

He left and so did I. We had a one-year plan. For the sake of love, I stopped everything destructive. I had found the one who I thought would change my life and fulfill in me what I always wanted and needed. The one who would show me my worth and let me see that there is a separate way of life. After all, he was a pastor's son. He was running from his call at that time. I did not even know what a call was. I just knew what he told me.

I remember my first night being home in West Virginia. I didn't know it then, but I do know now what I experienced that night. I remember laying down on my stomach to go to sleep and I felt an unseen hand gently touch my back as if a mother or father would do to their child to tell them goodnight. I felt safe again and I slept soundly.

Within 6 months, I had my license, GED and was a certified phlebotomist with plans on going for lab tech. Even with barely a 9th grade education, this was all so easy. I was advanced beyond what grade level I had achieved.

I talked every day on the phone and video chatted on Skype on the computer with my fiancé. We wrote each other letters and sent each other gifts. I was falling more in love with him because of the distance between us. We only had virtual communication and it seemed to knit me closer to him.

I was always leery though. His divorce was finalized but let us get real, I was always suspicious. I knew that there was always something to be looking for. I knew what people are capable of— myself included. I had never met anyone I could trust, and I sure was not one to be trusted.

I don't think he ever fully knew the change that had occurred inside of me, the commitment I had made to him, the purity of love and desire. This time I was all in and behaviors that were natural to me dissipated. They were vanquished. The desire for love to be met inside once again fulfilled those other desires.

I broke in his email and found out he wasn't exclusive with

me. I mean, really? Did I expect anything different? I never asked him to leave his wife for me. I was the opposite; I told him to stay and work it out. He had convinced me that it was years and years in the making and that he was done with her, with or without me. I remember the conversation when he called that night.

I immediately told him what I had discovered and when those words came out of my mouth a gut-wrenching cry came bellowing out of my belly. I dropped the phone and laid on the floor crying. I could hear the phone next to me and him calling my name in desperation. I could hear his voice breaking in pain for me. I'm sure now that he had his own fears of my lifestyle creeping back in and so he had his back-up plan. One big mess huh?

I grabbed the phone and told him I never wanted to hear from him again and that I wished he stepped on a land mine and die. I hung the phone up. For the next few years, he called me several times a day. I would only answer to cuss him out and hang the phone up. He was relentless, so was I. I had built a life on sand, so when the winds blew, everything went tumbling down. I did not know the rock yet.

# Chapter 26
## *Tragedy*

*He will wipe away every tear from their eyes and eliminate
death entirely. No one will mourn or weep any longer. The
pain of wounds will no longer exist, for the old order
has ceased.*

*Revelation 21:4 TPT*

 remember the call from the hospital. "Your mother has been hit by a car and we do not know if she will survive. She broke almost every bone in her body..."

I felt all the guilt of it. I left her alone knowing she did not have the mental capacity to live alone. I carried the weight of her issues for so long. Of course, I had to have some of the blame. One thing after the other seemed like I could not get a break. She lived physically but her mind only worsened. I was so used to tragedy and false hope that I couldn't bear another day. I was depressed beyond words and angry at the world.

I went to visit my mother at the rehabilitation center in

Florida. I went and spoke to the nurse at the nurses' station and for the first time in my life, I felt like someone understood the torment that I had endured. This nurse was obviously the attending nurse to my mother, and she told me that they had to move her to the farthest room in the facility away from everyone else. Her outbursts and delusions had become too much for anyone to handle. She asked me, "Are you the one that she says she raised alone?" I replied, "Yes." She looked at me and asked another question, "Has your mother always been this way?" I told her that she was much worse. Her response was that she did not know how I endured all that. I replied, "Yeah, me either."

My mother eventually recovered and went to live with my grandmother. It was not soon after my mother was hit by a car that I had an accident of my own. I was completely at fault, and it landed me a prison sentence.

# Chapter 27
# Awakening

*"And you will know the truth, and the truth will set you free."*

**John 8:32 NLT**

I T was not long in starting my journey of being incarcerated that I gave my life to the Lord. I had said that prayer before. Once again, I reached out to this God, I wasn't sure was real but I could feel a very real presence.

I was in a church service where this little blonde fire ball had come and preached at. For the first time in my life, I felt a tangible presence surrounding me that I had never felt before. It was so clean, holy, and full of love. I had never felt this warmth and purity before. I knew there was something to this man named Jesus and a Father that loves me, forgave me and had made me on purpose (or so she said). I still remember what her message was about—**Time**.

I stood up with a few other girls and we prayed the salvation prayer yet again in my life, but this night, I really meant it as

I called out to this tangible presence I felt. As soon as I got back to my cell, doubt, fear, and those vicious voices saying *no one can love and forgive you for all that you have done*, attacked my mind relentlessly.

I just fell to my knees. I shouted at the top of my lungs "God if you are real, I need you to hold me tonight." In an instant that same feeling came over me—only it was stronger. I felt two arms supernaturally wrap around me. Reality hit deep. There was a real God that had seen every moment of my life. He had seen it all. I had never believed in God. My thoughts were, *how could there be a God and I went through so much?* And *if there was a God, He is cruel, and I didn't want anything to do with Him.*

I laid on the cold concrete floor of a tiny jail cell, pouring out my heart and soul. I cried until I could not cry any longer. I did not know what to say. My whole life was replaying before me and a rush of every emotion imaginable came over me. For the first time in my life, I was completely laid bare and naked, with all my clothes on. I kept asking, "Why?" and then saying, "I am sorry." That was the two perceptions I had that night as I laid on that cold concrete floor of a jail cell.

I spent all my time learning as much as I could. I knew absolutely NOTHING concerning the Word of God. I was relentless. My fire and passion only grew, and I began to wax stronger and stronger in the Spirit. I was soon filled with the Holy Spirit, with the evidence of speaking in tongues. If I read it, I asked what it was and asked if I could have it.

I was not "churched". This made it easier for the Holy Spirit to work with me. Childlike faith and nothing to unlearn from religion, doctrines of devils and traditions of men. See I read about Acts Chapter 2 and the upper room. I did not know what had really taken place, but I knew it said they were endowed with His power. They were enabled to do things for God.

The next service I attended was with a woman. Her main ministry focused on being filled with the Holy Ghost with the evidence of speaking in tongues. I was filled that night. I felt His presence that evening in yet another way. I felt Him as FIRE. The intoxication of the Spirit overtook me as I yielded to Him. I found out quickly that every drug, drink, pleasure the world had to offer me was a counterfeit. He was all in all and He had pleasures and treasures I never knew existed. In Him I found my best friend, a friend that sticks closer than a brother. I found my true love. I found my acceptance. I found everything that I had ever searched for.

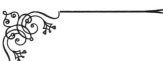

# Aware

I didn't notice the gentle caress of the wind.

Unaware of the soothing tones of the rain

Never stopping to smell the roses.

The sky looks brighter,

The air seems lighter,

Silk and satin never felt this good.

I behold the glow in the rainbow,

Blinded by splendor entering the windows to my soul.

Soothed as the moon vanishes making a disappearance,

Awakened as the sun makes her glorious appearance.

I find myself dancing to the melody in my heart,

Laughing seems to be my new interest,

My dreams are awake and alive.

Delightful is the taste from the fruit of my lips,

Encounters of discovery create a new script.

Cherishing the moments are essential,

Noticing has become what is valuable,

I am aware!

# Chapter 28
# Holy Ghost Boot Camp

*For all who are led by the Spirit of God are children of God.*

*Romans 8:14 NLT*

**T**HERE was an awakening that took place in me. I immediately transformed into Samuel the prophet. I heard the Holy Spirit speaking to me crystal clear. He called me by name.

After all, I kept hearing people saying the Holy Spirit was a person, so I constantly sparked up conversations with this person—the Holy Spirit. I was being taught that this Spirit inside of me is alive and that He was a gift given and He wanted to communicate with me! So, with child-like faith, I believed just that. He was for me, a trusted friend that wanted to reveal all truth.

"The Holy Spirit—because He is, after all, Christ's Spirit—is also a paraclete, a helper. Literally, the Greek word parakltos means "**someone who is called to come alongside someone else.**" In Greek culture, a paraclete was like a family attorney."

Let me share just a tiny fraction of what I feel released to share. Once I heard the Holy Spirit tell me to grab a jar of hair grease. He instructed me to pray over it in the spirit (which is tongues). When I did that and felt the release to stop, He instructed me where to apply it.

Just listen, I know I did not know what was happening at the time, I did not know what anointing oil was until years later. In jail, hair grease is as close as you get to possessing anything oily! I did not know what I was doing but I trusted Him and obeyed. As I obeyed His instructions, He graciously explained, "You just prayed protection over your cell." He even told me where to place the oil over the posts of my door.

I would ask a question and He would lead me to scripture to answer me. A question had been brought up during a session with a woman who was called to preach and teach the Word of God. There were many women in the session who had been in church and raised up by religion and tradition. So, I listened to what they said and how their dad or their preacher taught them this or that. I went back to my cell and asked the Holy Spirit—the real teacher—and He led me to the Scripture that speaks about how there is neither male nor female in the Spirit. It is not the flesh that ministers, it is the Spirit (or should be).

So, when it comes to the calling and gifting of the Spirit, He then said, there is neither male nor female. I said, "Thank you Lord because you know that I really want to be used one day by you however you would like." His teaching was good enough for me and oh man, it has trumped so many false teachings through the beginning years of learning truth.

I remember this time where a friend of mine had a brother that the law was chasing. He was intoxicated and in a high-speed chase. The Holy Spirit rose out of me and began to pray in tongues for his intercession. It was different this time. I felt the urgency and I did not stop it until I felt a lift. When it lifted, I told her, "Call now and see what has happened" The results? The car suddenly stopped and would not drive without explanation. I shouted and thanked God. We both did.

He was showing me the authority we have and the power of intercession early on. If I needed to make a decision, I learned quickly to ask the Holy Spirit and would not move until I felt peace leading the way. He taught me not to be lead of feelings, to only lead by His leading. Sometimes I would not get the answer until the very last second. This taught me not to be moved even by timing.

Just like the Scripture says, we should always wait upon the Lord. I was learning to cultivate my relationship with a living God— a present God. I would just know things about people (word of knowledge). I began flowing in the gifts of the Spirit more and more as He chose.

I began to learn about Satan and his demons and their work in the earth and in our lives. He began to show me demon spirits attached to people and taught me how to stand in the gap for their deliverance. This was vital in knowing the operations of the kingdom of darkness and the Kingdom of God. This is where I could take a step back and see how my whole life had been in this battle. How other lives were in this battle. How the whole world is in this battle.

*I was labeled as a statistic, but God was birthing me into a strategist.*

He gave me an image on this revelation; it was people with puppet strings. He showed me how we can be used for either the Lord or for the evil one, how I was a pawn for darkness and how the enemy used others as a pawn for his strategy. This is how I could learn to forgive others and realize that we war not against people, but the powers in operation behind them. This is where I could free myself from the wounds that had been inflicted.

Here is where I really had a paradigm shift. A spirit that does not have a body needs a host to operate. This revelation is where I understood that this illness that my mother had, was demonically controlled. Legion. So much began to make sense. My poor mother. My poor father. All these souls tormented and controlled by the powers of darkness and the effects of experiences in their lives.

The Lord showed me through a dream the demons and even the strong man. I will not go into detail here, but I saw a legion. They just kept coming and coming; endless amounts of them from all shapes and sizes. Then there was the one. The strong man.

But moving on, He taught me to pray because I asked Him to. He taught me to pray the Word of God and, He would just pray through me. I just had to get out of the way and allow Him to use me as a yielded vessel. I prayed before every service. If it was of God, I asked Him to give me ears to hear and understand, if it was not His truth, I asked Him to shut my ears, and He always answered me.

I prayed before reading any books that were of the faith to know if I should or should not trust the writing. He showed me early in the Word that there was deception and false teachings, so as a beginner, I just relied on His guidance and warnings of what to partake of. Yes, just that simple. I had this practice of praying before everything I consumed spiritually.

I feel lead to share what happened at a huge service we had at Christmas time. Of course, I prayed about the service before going and when the minister got up to speak, I heard the Lord say to me, do not listen to a word this man says. He began to speak, and it was all fire and brimstone. I mean, if I did not know any better, I would have thought I was going to hell sitting in that very seat. The man could not seem to get out of his mouth what he wanted to say. He kept tripping over his words and finally said this to another man with him, "Here take the mic, there is obviously no anointing on me for tonight."

Do not discount praying before taking in someone else's spiritual meal that they have prepared for you. Another time I prayed before service, and as I sat there, I felt uneasy. This time, He did not stop the service, nor did He speak to me, He showed me. I was enquiring of the Holy Spirit during the service. I had been feeling uneasy at her services. It was not until I was walking out and looked at the woman minister that in

101

the spiritual realm I saw her in the form of a wolf. Nothing had to be spoken, I knew that this was a false teacher—I understood.

I learned how to let Him speak to me. His Word, His voice, His people, His creation, His gifts and ways of communication were endless. He is everywhere all the time speaking if we are seeking Him. Asking for ears to hear and eyes to see seemed to become a daily prayer. Life even incarcerated became an adventure—a beautiful adventure. Every day with Jesus.

He would tell me not to eat for a certain number of days. I did not know that this was called fasting until I read and learned about it! I learned quickly that this is where I found a secret strength. I discovered that dying to myself opened me up spiritually to hear and see clearer and that the Word was my spiritual drink and food.

I had visions and visitations. I grew in knowledge. I waxed stronger in the Spirit. I was completely engulfed with the true lover of my soul. He is all I ever needed. The truth is the only thing sought after was Kingdom realities.

I was absolutely in love with this risen Savior that lived His resurrected life in me. I was in total union with Him. I was delivered from the nightmares I had been tormented with all my life. That was when I instantly began to dream. Jesus would speak to me through these dreams. I like to call this one of the forms of His love language.

He showed me things to come, also warnings. He showed me

WOMAN WITH A WORD

things to read and study. He would give me dreams about other people to help them. So much communication through this way of heavenly frequencies. I continued to study and read the Word, day and night. I began to watch what I put in my ear gates and eye gates. If it was not Jesus, I had nothing to do with it. He was teaching me the power of persuasion. The power that television and music had. He showed me how it fed the wrong parts of my flesh and how it would open me up for desires and practices that needed to stay where they were—dead.

He also showed me how magic is introduced in unseemly ways—cute little shows we all grew up watching. If we re-watched now as awakened believers of God, we can see how they are laced with many evils and sly witchcraft influences to bewitch young minds. Subtle ways to introduce things. Then of course, there are the full-on shows and music that are in black and white. No sugar coating. Murder, lust, fornication, etc. He gave me the revelation of how spirits are attached to this so-called entertainment. If God isn't the author, then who really is? I will leave this portion at that.

He told me I needed to be more adamant for Him and His Word than I was about my previous desires. So, I became that—a radical seeker. I was His beloved and His bride. His passion for me and my passion and pursuit for Him killed off my old self and the useless passions I once knew. This was true love. One that can't be taken away.

Early on, the Word of the Lord came to me while I was praying, "There are spiritual laws that I have put in motion, and

I have need of you." So, this whole teaching about how God doesn't have need of you is a LIE. He took back authority in the earth realm to give it to US. To exercise it, to put it in use. Not to sit back and just wait for the sweet by and by.

God had to take me out of the bondage of suffering in silence transforming me into: **WOMAN WITH A WORD.**

He revealed Himself to me in so many ways. I saw Him everywhere and in everyone. We are all made in the very image and likeness of Him. When He told me to love the SEED of His people, this forever changed my life. I honestly never realized that sleeping with a man before marriage was wrong— that's all I ever saw. For the lust issue I was asking help with, He plainly said, "Sarah, see them as your family". For me this worked. I had a different perspective and a different lens. Keeping a renewed mind was key.

I used fasting as a spiritual tool to train my flesh. I trained it in this area and learned to make the flesh listen to me and not the other way around. I learned what dying to myself and living for Christ was all about. If my flesh was trying to override the Spirit man, I ate less food and fed it more Word.

Subjection. I was tired of my old man, and I wanted nothing more than to walk out this new creation in Christ that He said I was. My spirit man was saved. I had to now save my soul. The only way to do that was to retrain my brain. The anointed spoken Word, prayer and my private studies. Did I mention fasting?! I think it is a critical part of our walk that we must adhere to.

Once the Lord gave me a scripture to tag to it that was and still is so astounding to me. It is a Scripture we hear spoken of mostly at funerals. To be absent from the body is to be present with the Lord. The less we feed this natural body, the more it dies and the closer we get to the Lord! This was a way of dying to self while getting closer to Him!

I stuck with what I was doing because it was bringing forth results. You can never argue a point with someone who has had an experience. I was experiencing freedoms I never knew I could have. I did not focus on behaviors and what not to do. He taught me to identify them; ask for His help and take on a new way of thinking.

The more I filled up with His Word and tore down old ways of thinking and allowed Him to give me a different perspective, these things began to have less power over me and less and less of my attention. One thing I will add that I have learned on the journey, is to never stop training. I learned this the hard way. Keep reading.

# Chapter 29
## Forgiveness

*"And when you pray, make sure you forgive the faults of others so that your Father in heaven will also forgive you. But if you withhold forgiveness from others, your Father withholds forgiveness from you."*

*Matthew 6:14-15 TPT*

THE very first process the Lord took me through was forgiveness. I read a portion of Scripture that spoke on this subject. I became so infuriated! I threw my Bible across the jail cell. I told God that this Christian thing was not for me. As I sat on the floor with my legs crossed and tears running down my face, that strong presence hovered around me and I heard Him softly say, "BUT I FORGAVE YOU."

My tears and anger changed to thankfulness and submission. I began my journey of forgiveness which in return gave me my freedom. This journey and process was never to point the finger at the other person. The Lord wanted me to extend grace as I needed it as well. The blood is good enough for me and it's good enough for them. Their debts they could never pay, and I should never expect it any other way. Grace and mercy came on the scene for the debtors.

The focus became about my heart condition. This became about me, myself and I. His soil, His field needed tending so that He could plant His seed, His Word inside a prepared garden so it could flourish. I asked Him how I could forgive the people I could not remember. I released a corporate prayer He gave to me through a book:

*"Father I forgive anyone who has hurt or harmed me including myself in anyway. I release them to you, and I sever every soul tie I have ever had in the matchless name of Jesus and through the power of His blood."*

He even began to give me names and faces through day visions and dreams. It would hit at random times. I would instantly say I forgive you. I felt these unseen chains falling off me. I was becoming lighter and freer.

I had to go in much more depths with some of my traumas. Still to this day God is digging deeper in me to pull out these nasty roots.

# Chapter 30
# Someone Prayed

*Confess your sins to each other and pray for each other so*
*that you may be healed. The earnest prayer of a righteous*
*person has great power and produces wonderful results.*
*Elijah was as human as we are, and yet when he prayed*
*earnestly that no rain would fall, none fell for three and a*
*half years! Then, when he prayed again, the sky sent down*
*rain and the earth began to yield its crops.*

**James 5:16-18 NLT**

I want to share this portion of my story to shed light
and to encourage. The Lord spoke to me about the
prayers of my grandpa. I found out the whole story
when I asked my grandmother years later when I came home.

The Lord told me that my grandfather's prayers is what has
kept me. When I later asked my grandmother about how he
prayed for me she said, "Oh Sarah, he prayed for you every
day." She said there were days he would stay all day in prayer
for me. She said that they would be in the middle of their day,
and he would say I have to pray for Sarah and stop whatever
he was doing and went in prayer. He prayed with diligence

and with fervency. His prayers kept me. Everyone included myself gave up on me, but prayer never did, and it worked and even to this day it still works.

I honestly believe he may have prayed out my whole life. There are times and times again that I cannot explain how I survived, BUT GOD. My grandpa was not only releasing the protective hand of God, but he was also birthing me into my destiny in those secret intimate times with God through prayer. Unfortunately, he never got the opportunity to see the manifestation of those prayers while on the earth. I know now that when you leave this earth one thing never dies—the legacy of prayer. Prayer never dies. Prayer is a part of your legacy.

# Chapter 31
## A Taste of Destiny

*It is the Lord who directs your life, for each step you take is ordained by God to bring you closer to your destiny. So much of your life, then, remains a mystery!*

**Proverbs 20:24 TPT**

I did not know how cruel the church world could be. After all, the ones that came to minister to us loved us and wanted to see us prosper. I was placed in an environment that did not give me a clear picture of the body of Christ and how out of alignment it really was. His (God's) family was dysfunctional as well.

I came home a totally transformed woman. I was as soft and sensitive as they come. The knife-carrying, fight-you-in-a-second woman had died. This new woman now wielded an unseen sword— the Word of God.

I honestly laugh now because even I couldn't understand the change. I asked the Lord why He made me so soft. I was as mushy and tender as a marshmallow. I did not have an outward fight left in me. My fight was done in the secret place.

Shortly after I was home, I was invited to a revival service. I was a little fearful of the unknown. What was next for my life? Could I really make it out here? Going to a service was where I knew I was safe and had a feeling of "home".

I remember standing outside of that small country church and I just looked towards heaven and said, "Lord I surrender my entire body to you." I went out in the Spirit for the first time and kept waking up under pews and had hands laid on me by the women in that church. I would get up and then go back out and wake up at a different part of the church; same women laying hands and praying in the Holy Ghost.

I came up different. I had found a new way of worship and warfare, in my shout and in my dance. God granted me a few solid friends in my new life. I will always be thankful for them. However, a lot of the church members ignored me and rejected me. I could feel it when I walked in the room.

I did not hide my past. I was very open and honest and shared my testimony. I was at a place I did not care what people thought of me, but inside I did not understand how they could call themselves Christians and totally reject true conversion. I started sharing my testimony in larger crowds than I was used to: churches, schools, youth groups, coalitions—wherever, whenever. I was on the news and in the newspapers. I remembered the statement I had made to my Father looking out of a tiny window in jail, "Here I am, send me." He obliged.

Within a year, I was heading to preach the gospel in Africa.

God sent me to another nation. He fulfilled what He had spoken to me in many of the conversations we had before. I went to Africa with $50 in my bank account. Miracle after miracle I saw God show up in my life. I saw there in Africa what I had always prayed for, what I knew existed—the true power and demonstration of the Holy Spirit. Demons were casted out; signs miracles and wonders took place like it was just another day in the office to them. I was at HOME.

I was on radio, recording in the studio for TBN affiliate television show, preaching a week revival. I was scared to death and did it all afraid and by the Helper—the Holy Spirit. He never let me down. He said what He wanted to say and did what He wanted to do. Mind you, I didn't have one sermon prepared. I couldn't get one on paper. He kept telling me not to worry, it is already inside of you. I didn't ask for the doors God was opening. I was just a girl who fell in love with Jesus and said send me.

I did not want to come back to America. The lack of honor, love and unity that should be in place as the Kingdom of God really isn't.

The Kingdom of God is not divided yet there are ranks in the Spirit; it is very organized. I love the church, but I was deeply saddened at what I saw. I asked Him what was wrong with His body, His church. His exact response was, *no honor*. God showed me who I was created to be for Him— a vessel fit for the master's use—despite how I was overlooked at home.

I fell in love with the land of Africa and the people and

located my spiritual Father. Before I left, Apostle Jefferson Stephen Okello and Bishop Aloysious Kiiza laid their hands on me and imparted spiritually into me. These dedicated and mighty men of God that are used to perform signs miracles and wonders even the resurrection of the dead. Men of God that had sound teaching and spent their lives in prayer and fasting. I felt beyond honored.

Who was I to have this honor to carry an impartation of their anointing? They charged me and released me to return to the United States with revival fire that was there in Africa. I'll never forget the words of Bishop Kiiza. He looked at me intently and said, "Sarah, you're going to rediscover yourself." I never understood those words until now.

On the airplane ride back, God placed a man of God, a Bishop from another country in Africa headed on an assignment for the Lord, behind me. For a moment we locked eyes and he then began to speak into me and my destiny. This Bishop released the very oracles of God to me for over an hour about many things. He gave confirmation to the things I already knew but never had spoken on because I couldn't comprehend these prophesies, they were too great, too big to understand.

Some of the things spoken were too much to understand and grasp. I was still trying to grasp the fact that God chose someone like me to fulfill His work here on this earth. These divine revelations were too big and vast for me to comprehend then and even now. Things that I will not share but will just choose to walk in and walk out.

I did not know what true warring for your prophetic was. Those Words spoken out of the mouth of the man of God and released in the atmosphere began the war— a war for my life and destiny. My spiritual covering, my Apostle, my spiritual father, was now thousands of miles away and I did not know what was lying in the days ahead. Though Yahweh is our Ultimate Father, He gives us mature submitted men and women of God to help guard and guide us as the Lord Jesus Christ enables them. This is where I will stop with that. That is for a whole other book. Let's get back to my story. I was never the same after my trip. I was truly awakened to purpose and destiny.

# Chapter 32
# God is merciful

*But God is so rich in mercy, and he loved us so much, that even though we were dead because of our sins, he gave us life when he raised Christ from the dead. (It is only by God's grace that you have been saved!)*

*Ephesians 2:4-5 NLT*

I was at a meeting one day and right after the meeting, I was approached by a woman with a big, beautiful smile. She went on to tell me something that I would have never expected. She said that her mother cared for my father while he was sick and that he was saved two days before his passing.

She told me the story of the nightmares he had. He dreamed of being burned and tormented every night. He would sweat profusely because of the pain he was in with the cancer that was in his bones. She said it took hours to get him to call on the name of Jesus. She even called her Pastor at the time to come over and help. She said it was at the tip of his tongue, but he could not get His name out because those demons tried to bind his tongue.

Finally, after wrestling for hours, he called on Jesus' name and she said instantly the sweat dried up and the countenance on His face changed. Two days later, he went on to be with the Lord. What a blessing it was to hear this testimony that God allowed me to hear. I remember all the hours I had prayed asking the Lord if He had saved my father and this day my prayers were answered. My God is merciful.

# Chapter 33
## Trials

*When you go through deep waters, I will be with you. When you go through rivers of difficulty, you will not drown. When you walk through the fire of oppression, you will not be burned up; the flames will not consume you.*

**Isaiah 43:2 NLT**

helped in starting up a women's home. I gave up my life and moved in to become a mother of the house. While there, I was lied on and hurt and pushed out.

I was the last person to find out the accusation. It was humiliating to know that this was circulating, and I didn't even know until I'm sure everyone else had heard it. I was shocked when I found out. I was literally jolted, but I forgave quickly.

I knew the power that unforgiveness held. I was not grasping why I was still being treated so disrespectfully. Instead of coming to me and handling the issue, it was a gossip fest. The value I had found in myself, others kept trying to challenge in many forms. This one was very personal though. I was mishandled in many ways. I loved them so much despite all of it.

I stayed in a place where all I spoke about was the old person I once was. I knew I had more to offer. Many people will only see you from where you have been. That is not who you are! It is vital not to stay there. There is nothing wrong with having a testimony and sharing your story. It was the story of others that helped me overcome.

Hear what I am saying, I had a story to tell but I also had so much more to say and offer. I always had an insatiable desire for what I knew was lacking around me. I knew there was more, and I had seen there was more. I was never satisfied spiritually. I felt suffocated by lies and pimped out for my testimony.

# Chapter 34
# Prophet without Honor

*Then Jesus told them, "A prophet is honored everywhere except in his own hometown and among his relatives and his own family." And because of their unbelief, he couldn't do any miracles among them except to place his hands on a few sick people and heal them.*

**Mark 6:4-5 NLT**

I moved away for a job. The job was amazing. I loved the work and the staff. After all, it was ministry and work at the same time. The director and staff seemed excited to have me on board. They knew who I was through social media. They even provided living quarters for my transition to another city. I was ready for the next chapter.

This move gave me freedom. As the word says, "There is no honor for a prophet in their hometown." After a while, I found out that they did not believe in speaking in tongues and the laying of hands amongst other principles. I found my-self laughing at most of my office visits (as I will call them). I would hold it in until I left with yet another discipline warn-ing. Once I could not hold it in and I busted out laughing right across the desk from my boss. Not in a disrespectful manner.

I loved her and I do not believe in degrading or ridiculing someone for their belief but this time, what she said absolutely brought out a belly laugh. She said, "...and furthermore Sarah, we do not believe in falling out in the Spirit here." I could not resist. I could not hold it back. *How on earth did they think it was happening?* I thought.

I thought to myself, *I just won't pray for anyone.* I cannot help that God backed up what I spoke. Did they think that I was knocking them out? I laughed for weeks. So did my other Spirit filled co-workers. Bless their hearts Jesus. I began to see more and more of the manifested glory of God whenever I would go to churches or conferences and teach and preach.

Sometimes He would show up in such a mighty way I would walk away in awe. I didn't try to let it show but I was just as shocked sometimes as the people. I was a seeker of the Gift-giver not the other way around.

# Chapter 35
# Sick as your secrets

*If we boast that we have no sin, we're only fooling*
*ourselves and are strangers to the truth. But if we freely*
*admit our sins when his light uncovers them, he will be*
*faithful to forgive us every time. God is just to forgive us*
*our sins because of Christ, and he will continue to cleanse*
*us from all unrighteousness.*

*John 1:8-9 TPT*

URING this time, my mother had run away from home and disappeared for a long time. When she called, I convinced her to come home. No one wanted anything to do with her, so I took the responsibility. I did not know that this guy that she was bringing with her was just as unstable as she was, and he was also an alcoholic.

I got her in a shelter, and eventually helped her find an apartment. Guess what? All that crazy was multiplied now with her and this new boyfriend. The perfect storm was already started, now the winds would begin blowing harder.

At this time, I had left the guy I was dating for a few years.

He didn't want marriage; he had been so hurt from his personal past. I had fallen into sexual sin with him. I was sure that we would make it right and get married. I had to move on.

After we parted ways, something urged me to take a pregnancy test. Positive. I took a few more. Positive. I was in shock and disbelief.

I went to work one day, and I remember standing up and the blood began gushing out of me. My co-worker looked at me and said, "Go to the hospital now." I went to the ER, and I felt like I was just in a whirlwind. I never thought I could get pregnant. I never realized the fears I had of being a mother because of my parents and experiences. I was ashamed of myself. There was a spiral of emotions running through me and I could not breathe. I could not contain the tears or the rollercoaster of emotions.

The staff treated me with extra care and that I will always appreciate. When all the waiting and the testing and the talks with the staff was finished, I wiped my face, went home, showered, changed my clothes, and went back to work. I lied of course about what really happened. I blamed it on stress. I did not know how to admit my hidden sin and the consequences of it. I was ashamed. So very ashamed of myself. I hadn't been able to process what had just taken place. I was stuck in limbo in every aspect.

I finished out my shift and put a smile on my face as I have learned to do. I remember that night like no other. I will never forget the sound of the rain that night. It was the loudest rain I had ever heard. It was pouring outside so loudly as if the heavens were in mourning with me. I mourned and wailed just as loud as the outside's pouring rain the entire night.

I was in anguish. This however was a different type of pain. A pain I had never encountered all my life. A grief I had never known before. I never knew a spirit of grief could grab a hold of you like it did, along with it shame and guilt. I never would have believed the next years I was about to encounter all because of the shame, the guilt, grief and my secret.

Wounded deeply, I did not know what to do or where to turn. I was afraid. I was embarrassed. What would they think of me? Now what did I think of myself? That self-destruction button was activated, and I did not even realize it until it was too late. This secret of mine was making me sicker and sicker. I fell into a deep depression; one that I could not understand or explain. I began to have thoughts of not being enough as a woman that I could not even carry a child. I had given up on the thought of ever being a mother. In previous relationships years prior, they had tried, they wanted me to have their child and openly admitted that they wanted to be able to always have me and a child that would tie them to me always. Sick, isn't it?

I had mixed emotions and now had all these questions of what it would have been like to have a child. Now weirdly enough, I had an unbeknownst desire to be a mother and was upset that this had happened even though it transpired the way that it did. I wondered what my baby would have looked like. I pondered on having the type of love that all my friends who were mothers explained to me—the instant joy that comes when you hold your child in your arms for the first time. A love that cannot be taken away.

# Borrowed Time

Gone to the point of no return,

Caught in the valley of death.

Emotional ties and lies were on the rise...

Sight without clarity

Numb without charity!

Here today, gone tomorrow,

In my womb now rests sorrow.

Silent screams echo inward through my existence,

Life fought you with resistance.

My choice my voice taken, replaced with cries,

They express what my thoughts can't describe.

Words can't explain this pain,

My tears flow as strong as the pouring rain.

Piercing deeper than flesh wounds can ever go,

Experiencing unfound emotions no one should know.

*A miracle instantly made then taken,*

*Leaving this moment shaken.*

*By my heart you were accepted,*

*Through my body you were rejected.*

*Blood stains, body pains are my memory...*

*My own body became your enemy.*


*Almost a mother, left to smother.*

# Chapter 36
## *Jaded*

*He gives power to the weak and strength to the powerless.*

**Isaiah 40:29 NLT**

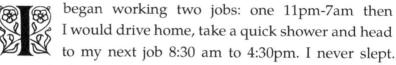began working two jobs: one 11pm-7am then I would drive home, take a quick shower and head to my next job 8:30 am to 4:30pm. I never slept. I never had time to do anything.

My mother and her boyfriend's issues were a daily thing. I was tired in every way possible. I was tired of my mom's episodes. I was tired of picking up everyone's pieces. I was tired of being in the middle of their toxic relationship and just trying to handle my own personal issues. I just wanted some relief.

I was gripped by grief, loneliness and exhaustion. Anger and frustration were now at the surface. I knew how to help everyone else but myself and my mother. I was just too ashamed to keep an intimate relationship with Him. There was a numbness I cannot describe. I didn't know how to pray. I didn't know what to say. I lost all desire to read the Word and could not hear his voice like I used to. I felt all alone. I was suffocated both inside and outside.

The battlefield of the mind was at an all-time high and I chose to stop training it. Those thoughts that I have been fighting all my life were back in full fledge. What was so wrong with me? Why do I have to keep trying to prove my worth? What was so wrong with me that no one really loved me unless I was meeting a want or a need? What was so wrong with me that I couldn't even carry a child? Thoughts of suicide were back.

I began to isolate myself. I was spiraling out of control. I had to hand in my resignation for the sake of my conscience and do what was right. I knew I had to walk away. This led me to a deeper darker place.

I had no fight left in me. I had given up again. I was wounded again. I had made wrong decisions again. Shame and guilt kept me down in that darkness. Those chains held me captive. I was afraid of what people would think of me. I was ashamed that I had failed my Father. I could not believe myself. I hated me all over again.

I took on burdens I could not carry alone in my strength. I was angry at God when I was at fault. It was easier to forgive others; it was forgiving myself that I had a problem with. Distracted and disengaged from the Word of God and with the spiritual tools left closed in the box, I drifted farther and farther away. Darkness began to beckon me, convincing me that I was a failure and that I would never recover. Suicide, yet again bargaining with me.

The darkness engulfed me offering relief. I placed upon myself that old familiar coat of shame I was so used to wearing. Truth had been sifted away from me. I now saw myself as a complete failure, worthless and damaged all over again. I had proven that I didn't have what it takes. My love for my heavenly Father, the seriousness that I had in pleasing Him had now become a weapon that I forged against myself.

He is a loving and forgiving Father, but I couldn't seem to forgive myself, so I turned my back on PURPOSE completely and told Him to find someone better than me; someone else to use for His purpose and plan because I obviously wasn't the one. I would never be anything just like they all said. They were right. I would never get it right.

For a long time, the only prayer that I could really get out in English was: "Forgive me" and "Help me Lord." Over and over sometimes a whisper sometimes a shout. When I did pray, it wasn't with understanding. I prayed in the Spirit in tongues. I did not know what to voice out. One thing I held on to was the power of praying in tongues.

He wasn't the problem. I was the problem—a problem that I would choose to remove. So, I removed myself. I still went through the motions of going to church sometimes, but I was just an empty shell hoping and wishing that eventually one day things would change. I could not release the failure to Him. I held on to it and the grief was unbearable. I went to sleep with it, I woke up with it I went about my day with it.

When my mother died less than a year later, another part

of me died. The grief I already had was now reinforced and grew in strength. Any ounce of fight in me was gone. I was tormented in a seriously abusive relationship. I had lost any sense of value. I was paralyzed. I didn't know how I got in and I didn't know how I was going to get out. There was a part of me that believed I deserved every bit of it, after all this was all I had ever known most of my life. I was pushed to the edge. I was back where I knew I belonged—in torment. The darkness had found its way back in. I prayed to die. I was immobilized and paralyzed. The inner child that was abused had the loudest voice in me now; coupled with the self-criticism of my adult self, telling me that I knew better.

The voices from within were savages, slashing me from inside out. The outside words uttered destruction. Voices I had heard all my life...a different face, same message. Death once again beckoned to me offering me a resting place.

I remember this day very clearly right now. My mind was on the Lord, there just wasn't much conversation at this time as I still held on to my failures. As I was walking in my neighborhood, I was walking with my head held down, strolling up a side street that is a one way only.

I was coming up it the wrong way when I heard Him say, "Look up." I looked up to see a road sign that said WRONG WAY. As soon as I locked eyes with the sign, I heard Him speak again "You are going the wrong way." I felt the Holy Spirit up and down my body and I knew exactly what He meant.

I escaped and started over. In time I got what I wanted and who I wanted only to have a broken marriage. More miscarriages. More betrayal. More regret. More heart breaks.

# Chapter 37
## Total Reset

*So we are convinced that every detail of our lives is continually woven together for good, for we are his lovers who have been called to fulfill his designed purpose.*

**Romans 8:28 TPT**

E try to find our own escape routes. We try to fit people like puzzle pieces into our promises and bring it to pass. We attempt to mark out the paths for our lives. We do not wait on God. I came to the rediscovery that **HE IS JEALOUS FOR ME.** I had to take a step back from everything and everyone and make a decision. First decision was to simply choose to live and to live for Him.

The harder I fought for my personal revival, the harder the enemy fought, but this time, I was not going to lay down. I decided I would have my new beginning no matter the cost. The more I strove for individual reformation, the more hell broke out.

My targeted prayer for a few years was simply, "Father not my will but thy will be done. Untangle me from every decision I made outside of your will." I may have swayed a little bit by the blows but this time I became the storm. I had regained my determination. I spent the requisite time gaining momentum. I did not allow the failures of a given day to hold me captive. I kept repairing and rebuilding and fighting all at the same time. A weapon in one hand a tool in the other. Like Nehemiah, I never took my clothes off and I took my weapon with me even for a drink of water.

While taking therapy once and even twice a week, I was finally paired with the right person to uncover a lifelong mystery. Sitting in front of me was a woman with an answer. These are the words she spoke, "Sarah, I believe strongly you are battling PTSD." I felt the Holy Spirit coursing through my entire being.

However, I only responded with an "oh okay" attitude and thought nothing more of it. Upon obedience of writing this book, I was washing my car outside and I heard the Holy Spirit call me by name in a very clear voice, "Sarah do you want to know what's really wrong with you?" This question resounded inside of me. I dropped my sponge and gazed up to the sky and said, "Yes Lord I would love to know what's really wrong with me". He replied instantly, "You've tried to self-medicate PTSD all of your life."

I saw in my mind a pyramid and at the top of it was this name that's been unknown—this hidden chief aggressor. I had identified and tried to fight off some symptoms but never the culprit. This active enemy that crept on the scene when I was a small child and was reinforced throughout my life by chronic trauma, leading me into cycles of dysfunction and fighting the biggest fight of my life to the point of suicidal ideation. I now have a name and a greater name to enforce against it. God wouldn't grant the enemy my life, so he caused chaos and wreaked havoc throughout my life, manipulating my interactions so that I would help him achieve his end goal—taking my life.

I am a firm believer in understanding the why of situations. This is a key many don't possess. Understanding is a form and level of deliverance.

My decision is final! The perfect will of my Father or nothing at all. His will is for me to live, to love and to finish. I decided to pair myself with His promise, His way. He didn't need my opinion or help in the process of promise. I needed to wait and not get in the way with what I thought was right and in my time. I did it, not for anyone but for Him, because He deserves it.

Not only does He deserve it, but He also desires for me to pick up my mantle I had chosen to lay down. I had to learn to forgive AGAIN. I had to HEAL again. I had to come back to my FIRST LOVE again. I had to rediscover myself again. I became jealous for Him because **He is jealous for me**. I had to do a total reset on the inside and on the outside. I learned to love life again. To love people again. I learned to love me again.

I already had the understanding that before I met my beautiful Jesus, I was trying to create escape and find completion in people and paths. I finally found my total completion in Him. I was not seeking completion inside of myself from people and paths when I decided not to wait on the promise. I was trying to control the creation and completion of the promise. I chose paths and people through natural sight and what appeared good…looking at time as my enemy.

This impulse to control to create and complete process of the promise only placed me in situations that almost brought to my greatest enemy on this side—death. The enemy had fought me in every area imaginable but none of his attempts were successful. So, he came in an unexpected way, he snuck in through the matters of the heart presenting options for God's promise.

Another revelation I have been graced with is that the fight for my life was an attack against MOTHERHOOD—what God has chosen to place inside of me. To abort bringing His glory to manifestation at all costs; that's what the enemy is after. To kill what you've been chosen to reproduce in this earth. Being a *Woman with a Word* is not just a catchy phrase. It is one of my mandates from God to reproduce another woman with a word. This is a movement. This is an uprising of the women of God to open up their mouths and SPEAK in whatever measure God has anointed them. Time to arise! This is a clarion call to all the women. **Will you be mothers for the Lord?**

I had to remove all the self-made promises—the Ishmaels in my life—in order to await the promised Isaac. I am still Sarah with a promise.

# I ECHOED DARKNESS. I NOW ECHO LIGHT!

I will close with the words of one of my favorite songs:

*I could care less if they don't sit with me*

*I ain't sitting with no misery*

*God prepared a table where there's victory*

*I could care less 'bout what they think of me*

*It was something that God seen in me*

*Make sure that you treat people with decency*

*I could care less if they don't clap for me*

*Hey, you can keep your flattery*

*I ain't got no time to hear no blasphemy*

*I could care less if they come after me*

*I said who cares if they come after me*

*Can't you see God's army in the back of me?*

*My king is supreme.*

# About the Author

**S**ARAH is from part of the Bible Belt of West Virginia. She is the founder and visionary of Royal Roots Global Ministries. Also, as an entrepreneur she now owns an apparel business called Sarah's Promise. Set on fire with zeal and passion to pull people into Kingdom realities. A true modern-day Deborah who has chosen to rise from the ashes to save a generation. She is called to the nations. Her favorite saying is "Everything that is good isn't God".

She can be contacted on:

Facebook @Sarah Speaks.
Instagram
Or her websites: www.royalrootsglobal.com
www.sarahspromise.shop